The Course
of This World

by
Edward O. Bragwell, Sr.

Truth
Publications

*Taking His hand,
Helping each other home.* ™

ISBN 10: 1-58427-214-7

ISBN 13: 978-158427-214-4

Truth Publications, Inc.
CEI Bookstore
220 S. Marion St., Athens, AL 35611
855-492-6657
sales@truthpublications.com
www.truthbooks.com

Table of Contents

Using These Lessons

1. Carefully read the lesson, using your Bible to look up all Scripture references.

2. Answer the questions at the end of the lesson. Notice that each item in the fill in blanks section is in quotations. These are quotations of Scripture either quoted or referred to in the lesson. All Scripture references are from the King James Version, unless otherwise indicated.

3. Version abbreviations used: KJV for the *King James Version*, ASV for the *American Standard Version*, NKJ for the *New King James Version* and NIV for the *New International Version*.

The Course Of This World

Introduction

One chooses between two basic courses for his life here on earth — the course commanded of God or the "course of this world." The Ephesians had formerly followed the "course of this world": **"Wherein in time past ye walked according to the course of this world, according to the prince of the power of the air, the spirit that now worketh in the children of disobedience"** (Eph. 2:2).

I. **The "World" Of The New Testament.**
    A. "World," in our more popular English versions of the New Testament is translated from three different Greek words:
        1. *Kosmos,* meaning "primarily 'order, arrangement, ornament, adornment.'"[1] Cosmopolitan, cosmetology, and cosmetics are examples of English words rooted in this word.
        2. *Aion*, meaning "an age, a period of time."[2]
        3. *Oikoumene* meaning "the inhabited earth."[3]
    B. "World" has several applications in the New Testament.
        1. In their application all three of the above words seem to overlap each other somewhat.
        2. "World" expresses several differing, but related, ideas in the New Testament. Among them:
            a. The whole world order (Matt. 28:20).
            b. The whole physical universe (Acts 17:24).
            c. The earth (2 Pet. 3:6; Rom. 10:18; Lk. 12:30).
            d. The Roman world or empire (Lk. 2:1).
            e. The world's population (Jn. 3:16).

---

[1] *An Expository Dictionary of New Testament Words,* W. E. Vine, p. 685.
[2] *Ibid.*
[3] *Ibid.*

     f. The present age and the age to come (Tit. 2:12; Heb. 6:5).

     g. The sinful element of the world (1 Jn. 2:15-17).

C. Ephesians 2:2 is a little unusual in that both *kosmos* and *aion* are used. Thus, the expression "course (*aion*) of this world (*kosmos*)" could be literally rendered "the age of this world."

D. Paul leaves little doubt about what is meant by "course (or age) of this world." It is that realm that is controlled by Satan, "the prince of the power of the air, the spirit that now worketh in the children of disobedience."

    1. In 2 Corinthians 4:4, Satan is called the "god of this world (or age)." Satan is the driving force that sets the standard of conduct for nearly all peoples and institutions in this present world.

    2. Since all (except those converted to the Lord) who live in the present world or age are following the "god of this world" in disobedience to the God of heaven, the term "world" is often used with a bad connotation. Of course, there is nothing evil about the physical world or earth itself — it is the human family, who has allowed itself to be controlled by Satan and his forces, that is evil. It is the course that the human family has taken in submission to "the prince of the power of the air" that is often referred to as "the world" in the Bible.

II. In The World, But Not Of The World.

A. Though Jesus' immediate disciples were living in the world they were not *of the world*: "If ye were of the world, the world would love his own: but because ye are not of the world, but I chose you out of the world, therefore the world hateth you" (Jn. 15:19).

B. Paul says that those "of this world" are those people in the world who are not "called a brother." Those "that are without" are of this world and those "that are within" are not. To escape all association with immoral people, one would have to "go out of the world" (1 Cor. 5:10-13). So, you have those *in the world* who are called brethren and are on the inside. They are opposite to those who are *of the world* or on the outside.

C. Christians are to live "soberly, righteously, and godly in this present world" (Tit. 2:12). At the same time, they are not to be conformed to the world nor to love its evil elements (Rom. 12:2; 1 Jn. 2:15).

III. "Worldliness" And Accommodation To Cultural, Generational And Geographical Mores.

A. One is not "walking according to the course of this world" simply because he may adapt himself to some of the customs and practices of his environment in this present world.

1. One does not have to reject modern inventions to "keep himself unspotted from the world." Those religious sects that reject automobiles, electricity, and other modern conveniences are mistaken about what is involved in the "course of this world." An automobile is no more or less worldly than a buggy.

2. One is not "walking according to the course of this world" simply because he may dress, talk or act, in some ways, like his neighbor who is not a Christian. Worldliness occurs when one *blindly* adapts to his neighbor's ways without considering whether or not those ways violate the will of God concerning dress, speech, and behavior.

3. The Apostle Paul, to some extent, accommodated himself to his environment in order to influence those he was trying to save. He wrote, "For though I be free from all men, yet have I made myself servant unto all, that I might gain the more. And unto the Jews I became as a Jew, that I might gain the Jews; to them that are under the law, as under the law, that I might gain them that are under the law; to them that are without law, as without law, (being not without law to God, but under the law to Christ,) that I might gain them that are without law. To the weak became I as weak, that I might gain the weak: I am made all things to all men, that I might by all means save some" (1 Cor. 9:19-22).

B. One is "walking according the course of this world" when he conforms to the customs and practices of his culture, locality, or generation *without regard to whether or not they please God.*

1. He may be so fashion conscious that he will conform to the latest clothing fads without asking if they conform to scriptural principles concerning dress and appearance.

2. He may take up the latest slang with no consideration of biblical principles concerning pure speech.

3. He may vacation at some resort and conform to the local standards of behavior without regard to "conduct . . . worthy

of the gospel of Christ" (Phil. 1:27).

Conclusion

The difference between "walking according to the course of this world" and not doing so is basically a matter of attitude. Those who are worldly minded allow the things that they observe in the world to set the course of their lives. Those who are spiritually minded let the word of God set the course of their lives. Their speech, dress, and activities are always tempered by a mind attuned to the will of God.

✍Briefly Answer

1. Name at least six ways that the word *world* is used in the New Testament._____

_____

2. What is the "course of this world"? _____

_____

3. Who is called the "god of this world"? _____

4. Why did Jesus say the world hated his disciples? _____

_____

5. In what three ways are Christians to live in this present world? ____

_____

✔Check "Yes" or "No"

1. Does God love the world? ❑ Yes ❑ No

2. Should Christians love the world? ❑ Yes ❑ No

3. Is Michael the prince of the power of the air? ❑ Yes ❑ No

4. Should a Christian ever conform to any of the customs of the people around about him? ❑ Yes ❑ No

5. May a Christian keep company with the immoral people of the world?

☐ Yes ☐ No

✍️Fill In The Blanks

1. "And be not _____ to this world: but be ye _____ by the renewing of your _____, that ye may prove what is that good, and acceptable, and perfect, _____ ___ _____" (Rom. 12:2).

2. "If ye were of the _____, the _____would love his own: but because ye are not of the _____, but I have chosen you out of the _____, therefore the _____ hateth you" (Jn. 15:19).

3. "I am made ___ _____ to all men, that I might by all means _____ _____" (1 Cor. 9:22).

4. "For all that is in the world, the _____ of the _____, and the _____ of the _____, and the_____ of _____, is not of the Father, but is of the world" (1 Jn. 2:16).

5. "Wherein in time past ye walked according to _____ _____ ___ _____ _____, according to the prince of the power of the air, the spirit that now worketh in the _____ ___ _____" (Eph. 2:2).

For Class Discussion

1. What is the difference between conforming to this world and adapting one's life-style to the customs of his times?
2. What do you think Paul meant when he said he became "all things to all men"?

Lesson 2

The Wisdom Of This World

Introduction

It is so easy to allow the conventional wisdom of the age to determine the course that we follow in nearly every facet of our lives. We look too much to the sages of this world to tell us how to serve God, how to live productive lives, how to rear our children, how to be happy in all our "inter-personal" relationships, etc.

There is no area of our lives, about which God has spoken, that cannot be made better by following what the Bible says rather than what the current conventional wisdom may be on the subject.

I. Worldly Wisdom Versus Divine Wisdom.

A. *Israel was rebuked for rejecting God's wisdom in favor of her own (Isa. 55:6-9).* God told the wicked or unrighteous of Israel, "For my thoughts are not your thoughts, neither are your ways my ways, saith the Lord. For as the heavens are higher than the earth, so are my ways higher than your ways, and my thoughts than your thoughts" (vv. 8,9). This was how things *were* with Israel, but it was certainly *not how things needed to be.* God's thoughts should have been Israel's thoughts and God's ways should have been Israel's ways. So, Isaiah pleads with the "wicked (to) forsake his way, and the unrighteous man his thoughts." When the wicked or unrighteous forsakes his way and his thoughts, God will have mercy on him and abundantly pardon him (v. 7).

The reason given for his need for pardon is that his ways and thoughts are not the Lord's ways and thoughts. Verse 8 begins with "for," thus assigning a reason for the call to repentance and the need for pardon outlined in the previous two verses.

Anytime one finds his ways and thoughts out of sync with God's wisdom then repentance and adjustments to his thinking are in order. The Lord's ways and thoughts must become ours if we are ever to please the Lord. As long as His ways and thoughts do not become our ways and thoughts we will remain alienated from Him.

B. *The Apostle Paul shows that the pagan nations of his day had rejected God's wisdom for their own (Rom. 1:18-32).* In "professing themselves to be wise, they became fools" (v. 22). This led them to "change the glory of the uncorruptible God into an image made like corruptible man" and to change "the truth of God into a lie" (vv. 23 and 25). Ultimately they sank into the most vile behavior imaginable (read vv. 26-32).

C. *Paul was careful to avoid all the trappings of worldly wisdom as he preached the unsearchable riches of Christ* (1 Cor. 1 and 2). He conceded that the gospel message was foolishness to many, especially the Greeks (1:18-23). However, he declares that "the foolishness of God is wiser than men" and that "God hath chosen the foolish things of the world to confound the wise" (1:25,27).

Just as Christ is our righteousness, sanctification, and redemption — He is also our wisdom (1:30). If we must look to Christ for righteousness, sanctification and redemption, then we must look to Christ for spiritual wisdom. This is why true gospel preachers insist on giving book, chapter, and verse for everything that Christians are to be and do spiritually. In spite of what Paul says here, brethren all too often look to worldly wisdom as they go about implementing the Lord's work in His kingdom. Paul refused to do this. He said, "My speech and my preaching was not with enticing words of man's wisdom . . . that your faith should not stand in the wisdom of men but, in the power of God" (2:4,5).

D. *James contrasts the fruits of the "wisdom (that) descendeth **not** from above" and "the wisdom that is from above"* (Jas. 3:13-18).

The wisdom that does not descend from above is "earthly, sensual, demonic." Of, *earthly,* Albert Barnes comments: "Has its origin in this world, and partakes of its spirit. It is such as men exhibit who are governed only by worldly maxims and principles." Of, *sensual,* he says, "It has its origin in our sensual rather than in our intellectual and moral nature. It is that which takes counsel of our natural appetites and propensities, and not of high and spiritual influences." Of, *demonic,* "Such as the demons exhibit."[1]

This earthly wisdom is characterized by bitter envy and strife or self-seeking (v. 14) which, in turn, produces "confusion and every evil work" (v. 16).

The wisdom from above produces good fruits and sets each in its proper order. It is important not only to see the fruits produced by the wisdom from above, but also the order in which it produces them. For example, as important as peace is, it is secondary to purity. Notice that "the wisdom that is from above is *first* pure, *then* peaceable" (v. 17). This point seems to be lost to those who are pushing the "ecumenical movement" in the world and the "unity in diversity" advocates in the church.

Within the framework of purity (in doctrine and life), the wisdom from above produces a spirit that is "peaceable, gentle, and easy to be entreated, full of mercy and good fruits, without partiality and without hypocrisy." The opposite spirit is produced by earthly wisdom.

II. **Brethren's Attempts At Utilizing The Wisdom Of This World.**

A. *The "institutional" and "social gospel" concepts are prime examples of brethren's attempts to use human wisdom to build up the church.* Many of the denominations, bankrupt of real faith in the Scriptures, have turned to social and humanitarian projects to increase their appeal to the carnal mind. Brethren, rather than patiently preaching the gospel and letting it appeal to whom it will, have often turned to the products of human wisdom in an attempt to get their fair share of those who would be impressed by such programs.

B. *Brethren, both "liberal" and "conservative" on the aforementioned matters, try in more subtle ways to use worldly wisdom to appeal to those impressed by such wisdom.* A church may have a special meeting, class, or seminar. The one conducting the affair is portrayed as being qualified to speak on his subject, not because of his knowledge of the Scriptures pertaining to the subject at hand, but his secular academics and/or secular expertise — which may or may not be related to the topic at hand. This

---

[1] *Barnes On The New Testament, James-Jude,* pp. 61,62.

writer is seeing an increasing number of churches using this tactic in their gospel meetings and other special efforts to appeal to the community. The speaker's fleshly accomplishments along with any prestigious academic degrees and affiliations are prominently mentioned in the advertisements sent out to the community. What is this but an attempt to use worldly wisdom to appeal to the carnal mind?

If one will accept the message because it is presented by one with credentials respected by the world, but would not from a "plain vanilla" speaker, his faith would not stand in the power of God but in the wisdom of men. Paul gave this reason for refusing to use the "persuasive words of human wisdom." The faith of his hearers must not stand in the wisdom of men. If there was anyone among the apostles who was academically qualified to appeal to those impressed by such things, it was Paul. When he did mention his academics, it was in a effort to down play their importance and value to his work as a preacher of the gospel (read Phil. 3:1-6; Acts 22:1-16).

Much of the current "how to" wisdom for pulpit and personal evangelism is nothing more than the wisdom of the commercial world. High pressure salesmanship that accentuates the positive in order to "close" more sales is at the core of many personal work programs and "pulpit ministries" — what ever that is. This may produce more and, sometimes quicker, "baptisms" (sales) than patient, persistent, plain, and complete teaching; but will it produce more genuine converts who are ready to stand up for the Lord even in the face of tribulations that Christians are taught to expect (cf. Jn. 16:33)? *All* positive preaching may attract and keep more of the worldly minded in the church, but it will not adequately deal with sin and error that constantly threatens the church in every generation. The wisdom from above says that our preaching must include teaching (not promotional hype) — both positive and negative. Paul even mentions the negative before he does the positive: "Reprove, rebuke, exhort . . ." (2 Tim. 4:2).

We need to be careful that we look to the Scriptures for wisdom in carrying out the mission of Christ rather than the conventional wisdom and tactics of the academic, philosophical, and commercial centers of this world.

The Christian's faith is not a blind subjective faith, but faith based upon evidence presented in the word of God (Rom. 10:17). In the pages of the word of God, we have ample evidence to produce faith in the existence and nature of God (Heb. 11:6), in the creation (Heb. 11:3), in the deity of Jesus Christ (Jn. 20:30,31), along with all the commands and promises of God pertaining to His creation. At times, it may be interesting to note wherein the research of various secular disciplines may corroborate the evidence of the Holy Scriptures, but the primary evidence for the Christian and preacher of the word must always be "what saith the Scriptures." To do otherwise is to produce a faith that stands in something other than the word of God.

We cannot allow the fact that the biblical approach may not appeal to many segments of society to cause us to turn to other approaches as our primary appeal in our efforts to save sinners and edify brethren. Churches are increasingly sponsoring events designed to produce and strengthen faith where the primary (and sometimes only) approach is scientific, philosophical, psychological, or sociological. They defend it on the grounds that their targeted audience will be more impressed with these approaches than with the biblical approach. What if some are technically persuaded by these approaches — where will their faith stand? Will it stand in the power of God or the wisdom of men?

Conclusion

"For since, in the wisdom of God, the world through wisdom did not know God, it pleased God through the foolishness of the message preached to save those who believe" (1 Cor. 1:21, NKJ).

✍️Briefly Answer

1. Into what did the pagan world change the glory of God?_____

_____

2. Name some traits of the wisdom from above? _____

_____

3. In what must our faith stand? _____

4. What did the Greeks consider the gospel message to be? _____ What was it in fact? _____

5. Why was Israel rebuked in Isaiah 55:6-9? _____

✔Check "Yes" or "No"

1. Does the Bible say that Jesus is our wisdom? ❑ Yes ❑ No

2. Does the wisdom from above teach that peace is the most important thing to the church? ❑ Yes ❑ No

3. Did Paul use his academic background to attract his hearers to his message? ❑ Yes ❑ No

4. Does being a Christian require a "leap of faith" even without verifiable evidence? ❑ Yes ❑ No

5. Must we harmonize our ways and thoughts to God's ways and thoughts to please Him? ❑ Yes ❑ No

✍Fill In The Blanks

1. "Let the _____ forsake his way, and the_____ _____ his thoughts: and let him return unto the _____, and he will have mercy upon him; and to our God, for he will abundantly pardon. For my _____ are not your _____, neither are your_____ my _____, saith the Lord" (Isa. 55:7,8).

2. "Professing themselves to be _____, they became_____" (Rom. 1:22).

3. "And my speech and my _____ was not with _____ words of man's _____, but in demonstration of the Spirit and of power, that your _____ should not stand in the _____ _____ but in the _____ of God" (1 Cor. 2:4,5).

4. "But of him are ye in Christ Jesus, who of God is made unto us _____, and _____, and _____, and redemption: that, according as it is written, He that glorieth, let him _____in _____ _____ " (1 Cor. 1:30, 31).

5. "But the _____ that is from _____ is first _____, then _____, gentle, and easy to be intreated, full of mercy and good fruits, without _____ and without _____" (Jas. 3:17).

For Class Discussion

1. Discuss what effect, if any, that the "social gospel" is having on the church.
2. Discuss some ways that brethren may be attempting to utilize the wisdom of the world in the work of the church.

Lesson 3

The Basic Lusts Of This World

Introduction

The world's preoccupation with lust is a well-documented fact. There are several New Testament passages that link the terms "lust" and "world."

> "Teaching us that, denying ungodliness and **worldly lusts,** we should live soberly, righteously, and godly, in this present world" (Tit. 2:11,12).
> ". . . having escaped the corruption that is in **the world through lust"** (2 Pet. 1:4).
> "For all that is **in the world,** the **lust** of the flesh, and the **lust** of the eyes, and the pride of life, is not of the Father, but is **of the world.** And the **world** passeth away, and the **lust thereof"** (1 Jn. 2:16-17).

Anyone who knows the meaning of lust knows that the world is given over to it. It is apparent on every hand.

Christians need to know both the meaning of the word, its implications, and the threat that it poses to their living soberly, righteously and godly in the present world.

I. The Basic Meaning Of "Lust."

A. Someone has said that lust is desire gone awry. In fact, the word translated *lust* is sometimes translated *desire*. Lust is undesirable desire. It is desire that is tainted by either misdirection or intemperance.

B. Of the word, translated "lust" or "desire," W. E. Vine comments:

> "Denotes 'strong desire' of any kind, the various kinds being frequently specified by some adjective (see below). The word is used of a good desire in Luke 22:15; Phil. 1:23, and 1 Thess. 2:17

only. Everywhere else it has a bad sense. In Rom. 6:12 the injunc-
tion against letting sin reign in our mortal body to obey the 'lust'
thereof, refers to those evil desires which are ready to express
themselves in bodily activity. They are equally the 'lusts' of the
flesh, Rom. 13:14; Gal. 5:16, 24; Eph. 2:3; 2 Pet. 2:18; 1 Jn. 2:16,
a phrase which describes the emotions of the soul, the natural
tendency towards things evil. Such 'lusts' are not necessarily base
and immoral, they may be refined in character, but are evil if
inconsistent with the will of God. Other descriptions besides those
already mentioned are: 'of the mind,' Eph. 2:3; 'evil (desire),' Col.
3:5; 'the passion of,' 1 Thess. 4:5, RV; 'foolish and hurtful,' 1 Tim.
6:9; 'youthful,' 2 Tim. 2:22; 'divers,' 2 Tim. 3:6 and Titus 3:3;
'their own,' 2 Tim. 4:3; 2 Pet. 3:3; Jude 16; 'worldly,' Titus 2:12;
'his own,' Jas. 1:14; 'your former,' 1 Pet. 1:14, RV; 'fleshly,' 2:11;
'of men,' 4:2; 'of defilement,' 2 Pet. 2:10; 'of the eyes,' 1 John
2:16; of the world ('thereof'), v. 17; 'their own ungodly,' Jude 18.
In Rev. 18:14 '(the fruits) which thy soul lusted after' is, lit., 'of thy
soul's lust.'"[1]

C. Today we tend to view lust in a too narrow context. To most of
us, "lust" has a sexual connotation. While the word is so used in
the Scriptures, it has a much broader meaning. For example, Paul
wrote that, while in the wilderness, Israel lusted after evil things
(1 Cor. 10:6). To learn what they lusted after, one needs to turn
to the Old Testament record of the event in Numbers 11:4-6:
"And the mixt multitude that was among them fell a lusting: and
the children of Israel also wept again, and said, Who shall give
us flesh to eat? We remember the fish, which we did eat in Egypt
freely; the cucumbers, and the melons, and the leeks, and the
onions, and the garlick: But now our soul is dried away: there is
nothing at all, beside this mana, before our eyes."
   They "fell a lusting" after fish, cucumbers, melons, leeks
onions and garlic! There was nothing wrong, per se, in their
desiring these things. It was the circumstances under which they
desired them and the behavior that they allowed the desire or
"craving" (NKJ) to provoke that made it lustful.
   Many folks who might not consider themselves lustful, may
very well be, in some of the senses that the Bible uses the word.

---

[1] *An Expository Dictionary Of New Testament Words,* W. E. Vine, p. 384.

Their "worldly lust" may not have anything to do with sex. They may be lusting for a week-end on the lake that would take them away from assembling on the first day of the week for worship. Or, they may be lusting for over-time pay that causes them to volunteer for work at the time of worship. Or, they might be lusting for that new purchase that would hinder one's giving as he has prospered. Remember that there are "divers lusts" or "various lusts" (2 Tim. 3:6).

II. The Big Three.

A. John divides things in the world into three categories: (1) The lust of the flesh, (2) the lust of the eyes, and (3) the pride of life (1 Jn. 2:16). These are the avenues used by Satan to tempt mankind from the very beginning.

In the Garden of Eden, Satan convinced Eve that the forbidden fruit was "good for food" (lust of flesh), "pleasant to the eyes" (lust of eyes), and "to be desired to make one wise" (pride of life) (Gen. 3:6). She, along with Adam, yielded to these lusts and brought sin into the world.

In the wilderness, Satan used the same approaches to tempt Jesus. He first appealed to the flesh by trying to take advantage of Jesus' hunger and urged Him to turn the stones into bread. Next, he tried to appeal to pride by getting Jesus to inordinately demonstrate His divine Sonship by casting Himself down from the temple's pinnacle. Finally, he attempted to appeal to Jesus' eyes by taking Him upon a mountain and showing Him all the kingdoms of the world and the glory of them (Matt. 4:1-11).

B. *The "lust of the flesh"* produces a variety of works (products or fruits). Paul warns against "fulfil(ling) the lust of the flesh" (Gal. 5:16). Then, beginning in v. 19, he lists the things produced by lust. He calls them the "works of the flesh."

"Now the works of the flesh are manifest, which are these; adultery, fornication, uncleanness, lasciviousness, idolatry, witchcraft, hatred, variance, emulations, wrath, strife, seditions, heresies, envyings, murders, drunkenness, revellings, and such like: of the which I tell you before, as I have also told you in time past, that they which do such things shall not inherit the kingdom of God" (Gal. 5:19-21).

Not only are the sins specified a result of the lust of the flesh, Paul adds, "and such like." Anything parallel to these things is included. One does not have to commit overt acts to sin, he may do so by harboring a desire to do so in his heart (See Matt. 5:28).

C. *The "lust of the eyes"* may also produce those works. This happens when the eye is the avenue for introducing the heart to the object of lust. Pornography is a prime example of the lust of the eyes. Lewd clothing and gestures are more common examples. However, *anything* that one sees that produces an unlawful desire falls into this category.

D. *The "pride of life"* probably catches more of us than we would like to admit. The American Standard Version calls it the "vain glory of life." It is this avenue that causes us to think more highly of ourselves than we ought to think. The Pharisee, of the parable of the Pharisee and publican, had a problem with it (Lk. 18:9-14). It produces such things as ethnic and economic pride. Peter was bothered with ethnic pride or racism, long after he should have learned better. His pride of life showed itself by his refusing to associate with Gentiles in the presence of certain Jewish brethren (Gal. 2:11-13). James warns us against economic pride (Jas. 2:1-10).

There are other prides that Christians would bear to watch. Such things as academic pride, geographical pride, family pride, etc., any one of which could cause us to be puffed up one against another.

Conclusion

If spiritual giants like David could fall to the lust of the flesh and the lust of the eyes, as he did toward Bathsheba (2 Sam 11), and Peter (Acts 10, Gal. 2) could be a victim of the pride of life; how diligent we must be to avoid being entrapped by the basic lust of this world!

✍Briefly Answer

1. What is another word for "lust"? _____

2. What "evil things" did the children of Israel lust after in the wilderness? _____

3. Into what three categories does John divide the things that are in the world? _____

_____

4. What is the meaning of "lasciviousness"? _____

_____

5. How did Peter demonstrate his pride of life? _____

_____

✔Check "Yes" or "No"

1. Does "lust" always have reference to unlawful sexual desire? ❐ Yes
   ❐ No

2. Is "lust" ever used in a good sense in the Bible? ❐ Yes ❐ No

3. Could one ever lust after garlic? ❐ Yes ❐ No

4. Is it right to show favoritism toward the poor? ❐ Yes ❐ No

5. Is it right to show favoritism toward the rich? ❐ Yes ❐ No

✍Fill In The Blanks

1. "For all that is in the _____, the _____ of the _____, and the _____ of the _____, and the _____ of _____, is not of the Father, but is of the world" (1 Jn. 2:16).

2. "For of this sort are they which _____ into _____, and lead captive _____ _____ laden with sins, led away with _____ _____" (2 Tim. 3:6).

3. "Now the works of the flesh are manifest, which are these; _____,

_____, _____, _____, _____, _____, _____,

_____, _____, _____, _____, _____, _____,

_____, _____, _____, _____ and such like"

(Gal. 5:19-21).

4. "But if ye have _____ ____ _____, ye commit sin, and are
   convinced of the law as transgressors" (Jas. 2:9).

5. "This I say then, _____ in the _____, and ye shall not fulfil the
   _____ of the flesh" (Gal. 5:16).

For Class Discussion

1. See how many kinds of lust you can find in the New Testament and
   briefly discuss each. (Hint: Look at Vine's definition quoted above.)
2. Discuss some sinful practices that are likely to have their root in the
   pride of life.

The Ethics Of This World

Introduction

Ethics is "the study of the general nature of morals and of the specific moral choices to be made by the individual in his relationship with others."[1] So, in this study we want to contrast the basis of "specific moral choices" used by the world with the basis taught in the Scriptures.

I. The Ethics Of This World.

A. *The "Great Thinkers" of the ages.* There has been no shortage of philosophers in history to shape the ethical behavior of a large segment of the world. Men like Socrates, Plato, Marx, and Dewey have had a great impact upon the world. Personal, social, and political codes of conduct have been based upon the reasoned conclusions of such men. Their alleged insight into life has influenced the lives of millions.

B. There are various theories of ethics or moral behavior that have been more or less systematized and named. These are taught and learned in the academic community and studied by others who are interested in behavioral science. Some consciously subscribe to one system or another, while others adopt the standard of behavior without having ever heard of it as a formal systematized philosophy. Some theories most widely used today are:

1. The *teleological theory.* To those who subscribe to this theory, the standard of ethical behavior is determined by the good that is accomplished. If one does a thing that results in good or was intended to result in good, then he must be on the right course. Sounds good doesn't it? But, we must ask, "How does one determine that good is accomplished? And good for whom?" One action might be considered to be for the good

---

[1] *The American Heritage Dictionary.*

of the individual, another for the good of the nation, or for the good of society as a whole. This standard of ethical conduct is based on an arbitrary and subjective definition of good. The one perpetrating the action decides what is good and whose good should be paramount.

2. The *deontological theory*. To the deontologists, duty is foremost in considering ethical behavior. Doing what is *just* is the right course regardless to what may be considered *good* by men. The problem here is that the deonotologist is the one who decides what is just and under what circumstances it is just. He has no absolute standard by which to measure his behavior.

3. *Situation ethics*. This theory basically says that which would ordinarily be wrong may be right under certain circumstances — especially if one acts out of love. In essence, it is the theory that one may bend or even break the moral code (whatever he conceives that to be) if the action is done out of love or compassion. Love or compassion becomes the higher law to which all other rules or laws must become subservient.

   This theory affects far more of us than we might like to think. When preachers begin to talk about how it was right for Jesus to set aside God's Sabbath law because of His love and compassion for his disciples in their hunger, then situation ethics has invaded the church. When a preacher is heard to pray, "Lord, we thank you for love. We know that love is the most important thing in the world. Love is more important than being right," one can see how deeply some are influenced by this theory.

4. "*Pragmatism*, (a) method of philosophy in which the truth of a proposition is measured by its correspondence with experimental results and by its practical outcome. Thus pragmatists hold that truth is modified as discoveries are made and that it is relative to time and place and purpose of inquiry. C.S. Peirce and William James were the originators of the system, which influenced John Dewey."[1] To pragmatists, if an act *works* for you, then it is *right* for you. The reason a thing is

---

[1] *The Concise Columbia Encyclopedia*, Electronic Edition.

wrong is that it causes you to experience undesirable results. Hence, promiscuous sex is bad because of it may produce AIDS or other physical damage or maybe even psychological problems. The emphasis of the pragmatist is on what the results of the action may be at the time, rather than any higher standard of right and wrong.

5. *Expediency* may not be classified as a philosophical theory, but it is the guiding principle that governs the ethical conduct of most people of the world. It is behaving in a way that is deemed to be appropriate for the circumstances at hand. It has elements of pragmatism in it. So, one lies, cheats, or steals at a given time because it serves his immediate purpose at the time.

II. The Ethics Of Our Lord.

A. *The Lord knows best.* He knows us better than we know ourselves and knows what is best for us for all eternity.

We are limited in our ability and wisdom. "The way of man is not in himself: it is not in man that walketh to direct his steps" (Jer. 10:23). Man left to himself becomes a law unto himself. Even "the way of a fool is right in his own eyes" (Prov. 12:15) and "Every way of man is right in his own eyes" (Prov. 21:2).

If the Lord made us, and He did, does it not seem reasonable that He would know what is best for us in time and eternity?

B. *Revelation and authority from the Lord versus philosophical experimentation.* What is morally or ethically right for us is determined by God's inherent authority and His revelation of His will to mankind rather than man's working out a philosophy based on his own wishes and experiences.

Jesus has all authority in heaven and earth (Matt. 28:18). We will be judged by His word (Jn. 12:48), according to the things done in the body whether good or bad (2 Cor. 5:10). We are told to "beware lest any man spoil you through philosophy and vain deceit, after the tradition of men, after the rudiments of the world, and not after Christ" (Col 2:8).

C. *Biblical love demands ethics based on Divine authority.* "If ye keep my commandments, ye shall abide in my love; even as I have kept my Father's commandments, and abide in his love" (Jn. 15:10). "He that hath my commandments, and keepeth them,

he it is that loveth me" (Jn. 14:21). "By this we know that we
love the children of God, when we love God, and keep his
commandments" (1 Jn. 5:2) .

The two great commandments of the law on love — loving
God and one's neighbor (Mk. 12:30-31) — have been abused for
years. Denominational preachers have for years stressed that
doctrinal rules, those rules that govern conduct toward God, do
not really matter as long as one really loves God. Now the
second great commandment is being treated in the same fashion.
This abuse stresses that moral rules, those rules governing
conduct toward others, do not really matter as long as one really
loves his neighbor. Biblical love demands playing by the rules in
our behavior toward both God and man.

D. *Did Jesus endorse situation ethics in Matthew 12:1-8?* Some
seem to think so. A close look at the matter should tell us
otherwise. First, the disciples did not set aside or break the
Sabbath law. They broke the Pharisee's tradition about the
Sabbath, but not God's law. God's law did not forbid all activity
on the Sabbath — even the Pharisees understood this (vv. 11,12).
The disciples were not *working*, as prohibited by the commandment; they were simply eating a meal. Eating was not forbidden
on the Sabbath. Secondly, Jesus did not hold David up as an
example of one whose unlawful activity was made right by the
dire situation at hand. Jesus plainly says, "It was not lawful for
him to eat" (v. 4). Jesus was exposing the Pharisees' prejudice
and hypocrisy by showing that they condemned His *guiltless*
disciples while excusing *guilty* David whom they venerated. Jesus
had already said, "Whosoever therefore shall break one of these
least commandments, and shall teach men so, he shall be called
the least in the kingdom of heaven: but whosoever shall do and
teach them, the same shall be called great in the kingdom of
heaven" (Matt. 5:19).

Conclusion

God made man, thus knows what is best for man to be and to do.
Ethical behavior must reflect His will rather than the findings of wise
men, unaided by divine revelation.

✍Briefly Answer

1. What is *teleology?* _____

2. What is *deontology?* _____

3. What is *situation ethics?* _____

4. What is *pragmatism?* _____

5. What is *expediency?* _____

✔Check "Yes" or "No"

1. Does love take precedent over strict obedience to God? ☐ Yes ☐ No

2. Is the danger of AIDS the main reason for avoiding fornication? ☐ Yes
   ☐ No

3. Did Jesus justify David's unlawful eating? ☐ Yes ☐ No

4. Can one really love God without keeping His commandments? ☐ Yes
   ☐ No

5. Can one really love a brother without keeping God's commandnients?
   ☐ Yes ☐ No

✍Fill In The Blanks

1. "O Lord, I know that the way of man is not in _____: it is not
   in man that _____ to direct his _____" (Jer. 10:23).

2. "He that _____ me, and receiveth not ____ _____,
   hath one that judgeth him: _____ _____that I have _____, the
   same shall judge him in the last day" (John 12:48).

3. "For we must all appear before the _____ _____of Christ; that every one may receive the _____ _____ __ __ _____, according to that he hath done, whether it be ____ or _____" (2 Cor. 5:10).

4. "If ye _____ my _____, ye shall abide in my love; even as I have _____ my Father's _____, and abide in his love" (Jn. 15:10).

5. "How he entered into the house of God, and did eat the _____, which was ___ _____ for him to eat, _____ for them which _____ _____ _____, but only for the priests?" (Matt. 12:4).

For Class Discussion

1. Describe some cases where you think people apply situation ethics to their lives.
2. Describe some cases where you think people are governed by expediency in their actions.

The Pleasures Of This World

Introduction

A fitting epithet for many fallen brethren might well be "choked to death." In explaining His parable of the sower, Jesus said that the seed "which fell among thorns are they, which, when they have heard, go forth, and are **choked with cares and riches and pleasures** of this life, and bring no fruit to perfection" (Lk. 8:14). The "pleasures of this life" is the focus of our study in this lesson.

I. Hedonism.

A. *"Hedonism, in philosophy, (is) the doctrine that pleasure is the highest good."*[1] Hedonism is derived from the Greek word, *hedone*, which appears five times in the New Testament. It is translated "pleasure(s)" three times (Lk. 8:14; Tit. 3:3; 2 Pet. 2:13) and "lusts" twice (Jas. 4:1,3). While other words are translated "pleasure" in a good sense, it is not so with *hedone*. Strong says it is "from *handano* (to please); sensual delight; by implication, desire: — lust, pleasure." Vine says it is "used of the gratification of the natural desire or sinful desires." Then there is *philedonos* — "lovers of pleasure" (2 Tim. 3:4).

B. One becomes hedonistic *when pleasure or even happiness becomes his main purpose for living.* Neither happiness nor pleasure are vices, per se. They must be kept subordinate to a higher purpose.

1. In Ecclesiastes, Solomon notes *the vanity of pursuing pleasure or happiness as a goal within itself:*

   I said in mine heart, Go to now, I will prove thee with mirth, therefore enjoy pleasure: and, behold, this also is vanity. I said

---

[1] *The Concise Columbia Encyclopedia*, Electronic Edition.

of laughter, It is mad: and of mirth, What doeth it? I sought in mine heart to give myself unto wine, yet acquainting mine heart with wisdom; and to lay hold on folly, till I might see what was that good for the sons of men, which they should do under the heaven all the days of their life. I made me great works; I builded me houses; I planted me vineyards: I made me gardens and orchards, and I planted trees in them of all kind of fruits: I made me pools of water, to water therewith the wood that bringeth forth trees: I got me servants and maidens, and had servants born in my house; also I had great possessions of great and small cattle above all that were in Jerusalem before me: I gathered me also silver and gold, and the peculiar treasure of kings and of the provinces: I gat me men singers and women singers, and the delights of the sons of men, as musical instruments, and that of all sorts. So I was great, and increased more than all that were before me in Jerusalem: also my wisdom remained with me. And whatsoever mine eyes desired I kept not from them, I withheld not my heart from any joy; for my heart rejoiced in all my labour: and this was my portion of all my labour. Then I looked on all the works that my hands had wrought, and on the labour that I had laboured to do: and, behold, all was vanity and vexation of spirit, and there was no profit under the sun (Eccl. 2:1-11).

2. *Solomon concludes that there is a higher purpose in life:* "Let us hear the conclusion of the whole matter: fear God, and keep his commandments: for this is the whole *duty* of man" (Eccl. 12:13). Life is not about finding pleasure and happiness. It is fearing God and doing His will—then happiness will find us.

II. When Pleasure Is *The* Objective.

A. *Pleasure or happiness takes precedence over morality.* Sin offers pleasure. The Hebrew writer speaks of the "pleasures of sin" (Heb. 11:25). If sin offered no pleasure, then Satan's job would be far more difficult.

When one gives himself over to the "pleasures of this life," he accepts pleasure wherever he can find it — sometimes in immorality. He may get his kicks from "lewdness, lusts, drunkenness, revelries, drinking parties" and such like (1 Pet. 4:3, NKJ). His highest aim is pleasure and these things satisfy his purpose. His question is not, "Is it right?", but "Is it fun?"

B. *Pleasure and personal happiness takes precedence over duty.*
There are certain responsibilities inherent in various relations that
we sustain. As children, we have responsibilities to parents (Matt.
15:4-6; 1 Tim. 5:4). As parents, we have responsibilities to our
children (2 Cor. 12:14). As Christians, we have responsibilities
to Christ and the church.

One whose life is governed by the pleasures of this world,
places his personal happiness first, then he will fulfill his duty in
his relationships as long as he can work it around his pursuit of
pleasure.

Why do we often see aged parents neglected by well-to-do
children? Why do we often see little children suffer need while
one or both parents are "living it up"? Why do we often see
churches suffering from a loss in attendance and revenue? Why
do we see personal evangelism and needed visitation lacking? In
all too many cases the answer is the same — the pursuit of the
"pleasures of this life." The week-end outing becomes more
important than the assembling with the saints.

C. *Pleasure and joy takes precedence over scriptural authority.* One
given to pleasure finds religion interesting only if it is fun.
Worship must cater to his pursuit of pleasure. Church work must
be geared to his pleasure. To him, the best preaching is that
which entertains him most. The best singing is that which turns
on his sensual response to music. The best worship is that which
"inspires" his sense of pleasure. So, churches in an effort to draw
and keep the pleasure-seeking majority of this world have made
it their aim to adapt programs of worship and work to appeal to
their desire for pleasure. Consequently many churches have
become little more than social clubs and entertainment centers.
The big question is no longer, is the church and its program
scriptural (read 2 Tim. 3:16,17), but is the church fun and
meeting the needs of those whose prime objective in life is
pleasure and happiness.

III. When Godliness Is *the* Objective.

A. *"The fruit of the Spirit is love, joy, peace, longsuffering, gentle-
ness, goodness, faith"* (Gal 5:22). Just as the works of the flesh
(vv. 19-21) are products of the fleshly or carnal mind; the fruit

of the Spirit is the product of following the Spirit with a spiritual mind. The objective is to follow the Spirit. One of the pleasant results is joy and peace. The Christian's joy and peace is "in believing" or "in the Holy Spirit" (Rom. 15:13; 14:17). Believing, following the teaching of the Spirit, obeying the truth, being in fellowship with God, being prepared for heaven are the things of real importance to Christians — happiness, pleasure, joy, peace on earth are given to them as a bonus. These things are the fruit, not the root — the by-products, not the real purpose of godliness. Had pleasure been Moses' objective, he would have remained in Egypt rather than choosing to suffer with the people of God (Heb. 11:25). His objective was to do the right thing, even if he must sacrifice "the pleasures of sin" to do it.

B. *Christians find pleasure in the strangest things.*
   1. They find pleasure in obedience and service. Rejoicing follows the initial obedience to the gospel. The Ethiopian nobleman and the Philippian jailer rejoiced as a result of their obedience (Acts 8:39; 16:34). The brethren of Macedonia and Achaia had great joy in service even in the midst of poverty (2 Cor. 8:2).
   2. They find pleasure in the obedience and service of others. John wrote, "For I rejoiced greatly, when the brethren came and testified of the truth that is in thee, even as thou walkest in the truth. I have no greater joy than to hear that my children walk in truth" (3 Jn. 3,4).
   3. They find pleasure even in sacrifice, suffering, and trials for Christ's sake (Acts 5:41; Heb. 10:34; Jas. 1:2; 2 Cor. 12:10). This is possible because of the hope that is in them (Rom. 12:12).

Conclusion

While Christians may enjoy many innocent pleasures in this world (even Jesus saw the value of leisure and rest — Mk. 6:31), their purpose in life is not pleasure but to serve the Lord. When they do this out of a heart of love and deep conviction it will produce a kind of pleasure or "peace that passeth all understanding" (Phil. 4:7).

✍Briefly Answer

1. What is hedonism? _____
2. What were some things that Solomon did to bring him pleasure? What did he find them to be? _____

   _____
3. What is choked out by the "pleasures of this life?" _____
4. What happens when pleasure becomes one's goal in life? _____

   _____
5. What are some things that should bring Christians the most pleasure?

   _____

✔Check "Yes" or "No"

1. Is one hedonistic because he enjoys pleasure? ❐ Yes ❐ No
2. Did Solomon recommend getting all the pleasure out of life possible because you just go around once? ❐ Yes ❐ No
3. Does sin offer a person any pleasure ❐ Yes ❐ No
4. Are peace and joy primary reasons for living godly lives? ❐ Yes ❐ No
5. Do Christians find pleasure in things that other folks cannot? ❐ Yes ❐ No

✍Fill In The Blanks

1. "And that which fell among thorns are they, which, when they have_____, go forth, and are _____ with cares and

riches and _____ of this life, and bring no fruit to perfection"
(Lk. 8:14).

2. "Traitors, heady, highminded, lovers of _____ more than
lovers of _____ " (2 Tim. 3:4).

3. "Choosing rather to suffer affliction with the _____of God, than
to _____ the_____ of_____for a _____ " (Heb.
11:25).

4. "I have no greater _____than to hear that my _____ walk in
_____ " (3 jn. 4).

5. "Therefore I take pleasure in _____, in _____, in
_____, in _____, in _____ for Christ's
sake: for when I am weak, then am I strong" (2 Cor. 12:10).

For Class Discussion

1. Discuss all the circumstances that you can think of that would cause
even innocent pleasures to hinder the Lord's work.
2. Discuss situations where churches seem to be putting the love for
pleasure above the need for scriptural authority.

The Riches Of This World

Introduction

Upon being asked, "What would you do if you had all the money in the world?", a man replied, "I would let it go as far as it would on my debts!" One does not have to have all the money in the world for riches to be a problem for him. He may even be extremely poor and have a problem with the riches of this world.

The riches of this world, along with pleasures and cares, are listed by Jesus as things that choke some who heard the word causing them to be fruitless (Lk. 8:14). Matthew's account refers to the "deceitfulness of riches" (13:22).

I. The Possession Of Riches.

A. *One may be rich and still be faithful to God.* Abraham was (Gen. 13:2). Job was wealthy and "perfect and upright, and one that feared God, and eschewed evil" (read Job 1). He lost it all, remained faithful, and the Lord blessed him again: "So the Lord blessed the latter end of Job more than his beginning: for he had fourteen thousand sheep, and six thousand camels, and a thousand yoke of oxen, and a thousand she asses" (Job 42:12). Joseph of Arimathaea, the Lord's disciple who buried Him in his own tomb, is said to have been a rich man (Matt. 27:57).

B. God *"richly provides us with everything for our enjoyment"* (1 Tim. 6:17, NIV). In this passage, Paul reminds the rich where their wealth originates, so they need to use it wisely, giving thanks and glorifying God with it.

C. *There is no inherent virtue or vice either in poverty or riches.* Agur, the son of Jakeh, said, "Give me neither poverty nor riches; feed me with food convenient for me: lest I be full, and deny thee, and say, Who is the Lord? or lest I be poor, and steal, and take the name of my God in vain" (Prov. 30:8,9). God, not being a respecter of persons, is not partial toward either the rich or the poor.

II. The Deceitfulness Of Riches.

A. *Riches can deceive one into a false sense of security.* The Bible calls it *trusting* in riches (Mk. 10:24; 1 Tim. 6:17).

   1. *Riches are insecure because of death.* The rich fool placed his security in riches (Lk. 12:15-21). Just about the time he had accumulated enough to take it easy (v. 19), it was all taken away from him by death. Now "whose shall these things be?" (v. 20) Paul warns poor slaves not to be overly concerned about wealth: "For we brought nothing into this world, and it is certain we can carry nothing out" (1 Tim 6:7).

   2. *Riches are insecure because of other destructive forces in this world.* "Lay not up for yourselves treasures upon earth, where moth and rust doth corrupt, and where thieves break through and steal: But lay up for yourselves treasure in heaven, where neither moth nor rust doth corrupt, and where thieves do not break through nor steal" (Matt. 6:19-20).

B. *Riches can blind one to his real needs.* The rich lukewarm church at Laodicea thought they needed nothing, but really needed virtually everything: "Because thou sayest, I am rich, and increased with goods, and have need of nothing; and knowest not that thou art wretched, and miserable, and poor, and blind, and naked: I counsel thee to buy of me gold tried in the fire, that thou mayest be rich; and white raiment, that thou mayest be clothed, and that the shame of thy nakedness do not appear; and anoint thine eyes with eyesalve, that thou mayest see" (Rev. 3:17,18). Do you suppose there may be churches today with their wealthy membership, elaborate buildings, and inflated budgets that may be feeling as smug as Laodicea?

C. *Riches can deceive one into a perverted sense of values.* Paul warns the "man of God" against this: "But they that will be rich fall into temptation and a snare, and into many foolish and hurtful lusts, which drown men in destruction and perdition. For the love of money is the root of all (kinds of, NKJ) evil: which while some coveted after, they have erred from the faith, and pierced themselves through with many sorrows. But thou, O man of God, flee these things; and follow after righteousness, godliness" (1 Tim. 6:9-11). There is hardly any evil known to man that men are not doing for the love of money while convincing themselves that what they are doing is not really that bad. The material gain, or potentiality of it, makes sin seem like the smart thing. It makes lying, cheating, and stealing seem trivial to many.

The remote possibility of "hitting it big" deceives many into wasting God's material blessings on gambling — telling themselves that it is just an innocent pastime. Gambling is far from innocent. It violates basic Bible principles such as good stewardship (cf. Lk. 15:13), the "golden rule" (Matt. 7:12), exploiting others (Jas. 5:1-5), to name just a few. Its fruits are not good. It has proven to be addictive to the point that men and women will do it regardless of how it affects their financial and moral responsibilities to themselves and those they profess to love. They will often resort to other immoral and unlawful means to support their habit or increase their odds. It has much the same effect that alcoholism has on the lives of those associated with the alcoholic.

D. *Riches can blind one to moral and spiritual responsibilities.* This can affect both the "have's" and the "have not's."

1. An employee, working for a rich employer, can easily convince himself to help himself to that which belongs to his employer because, after all, he has so much that he would never miss it. This is called "purloining" (KJV, ASV), "pilfering" (NKJ), or "steal(ing)" (NIV) in the Bible (Tit. 2:10). It is not living soberly, righteously, and godly in this present world (v. 12). He may even tell himself that he deserves what he is taking for all the hard work he has given the company.

He may even think that it is alright to loaf on the job, while receiving full pay, as long as he can get away with it. When he does this he violates a basic Bible principle: "Servants, obey in all things your masters according to the flesh; not with eyeservice, as menpleasers; but in singleness of heart, fearing God" (Col. 3:22). He may convince himself that this practice is not all that bad because nearly everyone does it. Besides what the boss doesn't know can't hurt him.

2. An employer may take advantage of an employee by not

paying him as he should. He may even deceive himself into thinking that it is just good business or stewardship. James wrote, "Behold, the hire of the labourers who have reaped down your fields, which is of you kept back by fraud, crieth: and the cries of them which have reaped are entered into the ears of the Lord of sabaoth" (Jas. 5:4).

3. A child may withhold needed support from his parents out of greed and find ways to justify it in his own mind (cf. Matt. 15:4-6).

4. Children of God may, through covetousness, rob God of that portion of their prosperity they should be giving back (cf. Mal. 3:8). They may even convince themselves that there is good reason for it. Christians have a responsibility to give liberally (read also 1 Cor. 16:1,2; 2 Cor 8 and 9).

5. A Christians may *voluntarily* accept extra work, even if it means missing church services and convince himself it is justified — after all, can't we all use more money? We need enough faith to believe that by putting the kingdom of God first that we will be provided with opportunity to acquire what we really need to live without neglecting spiritual duties (cf. Matt. 6:33).

Conclusion

While we must have money to get along in this world, we need to know the evils that are often associated with it. We need to acquire and retain it honestly, use it wisely, and seek to understand its benefits and limitations. Let us thank God for what He gives us and use it to his glory. Let us be more interested in "unsearchable riches" (Eph. 3:8), "treasures in heaven" (Matt. 6:20), and being rich in faith and good works (Jas. 2:5; 1 Tim. 6:18).

✍Briefly Answer

1. Who were some rich people in the Bible who were faithful to God? _

2. What are some dangers associated with both riches and poverty? ___

3. Which New Testament church thought that it needed nothing because

it was rich? _____

4. Why can riches not provide us with real security? _____

_____

5. What are some scriptural principles associated with gambling? _____

_____

✔Check "Yes" or "No"

1. Was the rich fool condemned because he was rich? ☐ Yes ☐ No

2. Is money the root of all kinds of evil? ☐ Yes ☐ No

3. Is it possible to rob God? ☐ Yes ☐ No

4. Does God promise to reward all the faithful with good health and material wealth? ☐ Yes ☐ No

5. Is it right for an employee to compensate for his employer's refusal to pay him just wages by taking enough of the employer's goods to make up the difference? ☐ Yes ☐ No

✎Fill In The Blanks

1. "So the Lord _____ the latter end of Job more than his _____: for he had _____ _____ sheep, and six thousand _____, and a _____ yoke of oxen, and a _____ she asses" (Job 42:12).

2. "But lay up for yourselves _____ in heaven, where neither _____ nor _____ doth corrupt, and where _____ do not _____ _____ ____ _____" (Matt. 6:19).

3. "Behold, the _____ of the labourers who have reaped down your
   fields, which is of you kept back by _____, crieth: and the cries
   of them which have reaped are entered into the ears of the _____
   of sabaoth" (Jas. 5:4).

4. "Upon the first day of the week let every one of you _____ _____
   _____ _____, as God hath _____ him, that there be no
   gatherings when I come" (1 Cor. 16:2).

5. "That they do good, that they be _____ in _____ works,
   _____to distribute, willing to _____" (1 Tim. 6:18).

For Class Discussion

1. Discuss situations where Christians may allow the riches of this world
   to pull them down spiritually.
2. Discuss all the evils that you can think of that may be rooted in the
   love of money.

Lesson 7

The Cares Of This World

Introduction

Like Martha, too many of us are "careful and troubled about many things" (Lk. 10:41). The "cares of this world" hinder many from being fruitful in the kingdom of God (Matt. 13:22, NKJ). The cares of this world absorb so much time and energy that could be devoted to productive service in the Lord's vineyard. In some cases people are completely disabled by them. We need to know more about these cares so that we can better cope with them.

I. Understanding The Cares Of This World.

   A. *"Care" and "careful," in the New Testament, are often other words for "anxiety" and "anxious."* The original words are *merimna* and *merimnao*. Of *merimna*, Vine says, "probably connected with *merizo*, 'to draw in different directions, distract,' hence signifies 'that which causes this, a care, especially an anxious care.'" Of *merimnao*, he says, "signifies 'to be anxious about, to have a distracting care.'"[1] Hence, the kind of care condemned in the New Testament is that anxious care that distracts one from duty, especially duty in the Lord's work.

   B. *Not all care or even anxiety is bad.* Paul commends the Philippians for being careful for his welfare (Phil. 4:10). Here "careful" means great concern and is translated from a different word from those above. However, the two words above are used by Paul to express a care or anxiety that is good. "That there should be no schism in the body; but that the members should have the same care (*merimnao*) one for another" (1 Cor 12:25). "Beside those things that are without, that which cometh upon me daily, the

---

[1]*An Expository Dictionary Of New Testament Words.* W. E. Vine, p. 89.

care (*merimna*) of all the churches (2 Cor 11:28). "For I have no man likeminded, who will naturally care (*merimnao*) for your state" (Phil 2:20). If more Christians were careful or anxious for one another, the welfare of "all the churches" and for the state of their brethren, there is no telling how effective we could be in doing the Lord's work in the world.

II. Common Cares Of This World.
A. *Anxiety over the necessities of life.* Jesus addresses this problem in the Sermon on the Mount:

> Therefore I say to you, do not worry about your life, what you will eat or what you will drink; nor about your body, what you will put on. Is not life more than food and the body more than clothing? Look at the birds of the air, for they neither sow nor reap nor gather into barns; yet your heavenly Father feeds them. Are you not of more value than they? Which of you by worrying can add one cubit to his stature? So why do you worry about clothing? Consider the lilies of the field, how they grow: they neither toil nor spin; and yet I say to you that even Solomon in all his glory was not arrayed like one of these. Now if God so clothes the grass of the field, which today is, and tomorrow is thrown into the oven, will He not much more clothe you, O you of little faith? Therefore do not worry, saying, "What shall we eat?" or "What shall we drink?" or "What shall we wear?" For after all these things the Gentiles seek. For your heavenly Father knows that you need all these things (Matt. 6:25-32, NKJ).

Because the King James Version uses "take no thought" where others translations have used "worry" or "anxious," some are puzzled about the Lord's meaning. Surely we have to take some thought about food, clothing, and shelter. Jesus is not saying never think about it or plan for it. It is the distracting thought or anxiety that He condemns.

B. *Anxiety over the future.* Jesus said, "Do not worry about tomorrow, for tomorrow will worry about its own things. Sufficient for the day is its own trouble" (Matt. 6:34, NKJ). How much energy and time do you suppose we waste annually worrying and fretting about what *might* happen, or what *could* happen or even what *will* happen in the future—none of which we can do anything about? Even if it is something we can do something about, we do not need to let it distract us from our present responsibilities. We have enough present trouble to keep us busy without borrowing from tomorrow. If there is something you can do today that would help tomorrow's possible situation, then do it today and stop worrying about it.

C. *Anxiety over many things.* Martha's care or anxiety (*merimnao*) was not over the future nor even the necessities of life. She was allowing care for the immediate things of lesser importance to overshadow and distract her from the "one thing needful" (Lk. 10:41,42). The New King James says that "Martha was distracted with much serving" (v. 40). Do you think that we might be distracted by much serving? We have to serve the little league, serve the civic club, serve the job, serve the school, serve recreation, serve at social functions, etc. until we choke out the "one thing needful."

Was it wrong, per se, for Martha to be busy with serving? No! But, she should not be so involved that it distracted her from greater service. Nor should we.

III. Coping With Cares Of This World.

A. *By strengthening our faith.* Jesus indicates that anxiety over such things as food and clothing could be traced to a lack of faith. He said, "O ye of little faith" (Matt. 6:30). If God could clothe the lilies better than even Solomon in all his glory was clothed (v. 29), if God clothes the grass that is so soon cut down (30), and if He takes care of the birds of the air (v. 26) — surely we can believe that He will find a way to take care of our needs without our having to be so anxious about them.

Since faith comes from hearing the word of God (Rom. 10:17), we can strengthen our faith by spending more time reading, studying and meditating upon it. Our faith is further strengthened as we exercise it from day to day (cf. 1 Pet. 1:7).

B. *By prayer and thanksgiving.* "Be careful (anxious, NKJ) for nothing; but in every thing by prayer and supplication with thanksgiving let your requests be made known unto God" (Phil. 4:6). It is harder to worry about things while one is counting his blessings so that he can give thanks to God for them.

C. *By proper thinking.* "Finally, brethren, whatever things are true, whatever things are noble, whatever things are just, whatever things are pure, whatever things are lovely, whatever things are of good report, if there is any virtue and if there is anything praiseworthy — meditate on these things" (Phil. 4:8, NKJ). *The Twentieth Century New Testament* says, "let your thoughts dwell on these things."

D. *By depositing our cares with God.* "Humble yourselves therefore under the mighty hand of God, that he may exalt you in due time: Casting all your care upon him; for he careth for you" (1 Pet. 5:6,7). The word for *casting* is the word used in Luke 19:35 — "they cast their garments upon the colt." The idea is that of casting our cares (the things we are anxious about) upon the Lord and letting Him carry the load.

E. *By letting tomorrow take care of itself* (Matt. 6:34). Someone has said, "We may not know what tomorrow holds, but we do know Him who holds tomorrow."

F. *By seeking first the kingdom of God and His righteousness.* This is the antidote that Jesus gave for anxiety (Matt. 6:33). If we will do this we will be much less concerned about the future and temporal things. Our main concern will be for the kingdom of God and His righteousness, thus minimizing our concern for other things.

Conclusion

The cares of this world can be overcome—if we will "set our affections on things above, not on things on the earth" (Col. 3:2).

✍Briefly Answer

1. What was Martha's problem? _____

2. What examples of God's care did Jesus use to show that His disciples need not be anxious about the necessities of life? _____

_____

3. What are some ways one can cope with the cares of this world? ____

_____

4. What are some good anxieties? _____

5. What antidote did Jesus give for anxiety? _____

✔Check "Yes" or "No"

1. Should we think about tomorrow at all? ❒ Yes ❒ No

2. Should Christians ever be anxious for each other's welfare? ❒ Yes

❒ No

3. Do prayer and thanksgiving help us overcome the cares of this world?

❒ Yes ❒ No

4. Does faith come by a special anointing of the Holy Spirit? ❒ Yes

❒ No

5. Does needless anxiety show a lack of faith? ❒ Yes ❒ No

✍Fill In The Blanks

1. "And _____ answered and said unto her, Martha, Martha, thou
art _____ and _____ about many things" (Lk. 10:41).

2. "But seek ye _____ the _____ of God, and his
_____; and all these things shall be _____ ___
_____" (Matt. 6:33).

3. "Be _____ for nothing; but in every thing by _____ and
supplication with _____ let your requests be made
known unto God" (Phil. 4:6).

4. "Casting all your _____ upon him; for he _____ for you"
(1 Pet. 5:7).

5. "Beside those things that are _____, that which cometh upon me

_____, the _____ of all the churches" (2 Cor. 11:28).

For Class Discussion

1. How is the church hindered by the cares of this world?
2. How may anxiety affect a person in his daily life?

The Fashions Of This World

Introduction

As one can see from this dictionary definition, "fashion" has a variety of connotations:

—n. 1. The way in which something is formed; configuration. 2. Kind or variety; sort. 3. A manner of performing; way: Do it in this fashion. 4. The current style or custom, as in dress or behavior: out of fashion. 5. A piece of clothing that is in the current mode. 6. The manners, customs, and mode of life characteristic of the upper classes.[1]

When the Bible speaks of the "fashion of this world" (1 Cor. 7:31, KJV, ASV) it is speaking of it in the sense of the first meaning, i.e., the *form* of this world (NKJ). However, an important part of the "fashion of this world" to many are the *fashions* of this world, using the word as in the fifth meaning of the dictionary given above—"a piece of clothing that is in the current mode."

Christians are told not to be "fashioning yourselves according to the former lusts in your ignorance" (1 Pet 1:14). This, no doubt, is speaking of conforming to the world in general. However, a part of that "fashioning" has to do with many "fashions" that are popularly worn by people of the world — and often blindly adopted by Christians. Too many merely reflect the "current mode" or popular styles surrounding personal appearance rather than moving cautiously by viewing them in the light of scriptural principles governing a Christian's appearance and behavior.

I. Styles Send Signals.

A. *Clothes may not make the man, but they do reflect the man.* The

---

[1] *The American Heritage Dictionary*, Electronic Edition.

way that people adorn themselves tells the world *something* about them. What it tells may or may not be of any real significance. The two men considered in James 2:1-9 signaled to all their economic, and probable social, standing in the world. In this passage, both the poor and rich are identified by their personal appearance. The prosperous man was identified by his "gold ring and fine clothes," while the poor man was identified by his "shabby clothes" (v. 2, NIV). In this case the difference reflected by their appearance must make no difference. One's standing before God does not depend on his economic or social standing in this world — nor should it affect our treatment of him. However, even though the passage shows that it should not make any difference, it also shows that personal appearance does reflect something about a person. While it makes no difference whether one is rich or poor, there are things about people that do make a difference that are often reflected by the way they adorn themselves.

B. *One may signal an attitude toward an occasion* by the way he dresses for it. When Joseph was to appear before the king of Egypt, he dressed accordingly. The Bible says, "He shaved himself, and changed his raiment, and came in unto Pharaoh" (Gen. 41:14). He showed enough respect for Pharaoh's position to not go with "just what he happened to have on." In the parable of the wedding garment, a man showed up at the wedding without dressing appropriately for the occasion (Matt. 22:11,12). These two cases illustrate how one's dress reflects his attitude toward an event. This raises some questions for us about the public assembly to worship the Lord. Do we consider it a very special event or just another casual gathering? What does our dress suggest about our attitude toward it? The religious people of the world may treat worship casually, but should those who worship God in spirit and truth approach it in such fashion?

C. *One may signal certain character traits* by his manner of dress. Most of us have seen people dressed in a way that may suggest laziness and/or carelessness. One's adornment may signal ungodliness. There is such a thing as "the attire of a harlot" or "dressed like a prostitute" (Prov. 7:10, KJV, NIV). On the other hand, one may signal godliness by being dressed as "becometh women professing godliness" (1 Tim. 2:10).

II. Signals Christians Need To Send.

A. *Christians need to be seen as lights* in the midst of the moral and spiritual darkness of this world (Matt. 5:16; Phil. 2:15). As such, they need to emit clearly and unmistakably an image of godliness. If they do not adorn themselves as ones professing godliness, they cannot have the influence they otherwise would. The vast majority of those who design the fashions of this world have little interest in reflecting "good works," as the Bible would define them; therefore their creations, more often than not, tend to reflect sensuality rather than spirituality. We should be aware of this and be cautious about adopting every fad of fashion that might come along.

B. *Christians should show respect for God's ordained "gender-gap."* God has given men and women different roles and those roles need to be reflected in their appearance. The Bible says, "Doth not even nature itself teach you, that, if a man have long hair, it is a shame unto him? But if a woman have long hair, it is a glory to her" (1 Cor. 11:14,15). In the Old Testament there seems to have been garments pertaining to men and those pertaining to women (Deut. 22:5). Do not these principles suggest that men and women should adorn themselves in a way that shows all that they honor the differences that God has placed between men and women — regardless of what the current fashions of the world might dictate?

C. *Christians should show that they are governed by modesty, propriety, and moderation.* One's personal appearance, more often than not, is a visual indication of the presence or absence of these inner virtues. "In like manner also, that the women adorn themselves in modest apparel, with propriety and moderation, not with braided hair or gold or pearls or costly clothing, but, which is proper for women professing godliness, with good works" (1 Tim. 2:9,10 NKJ). One needs to look at the meaning of three keys words in verse 9. Here they are with W.E. Vine's definitions:

Modest

kosmios — "orderly, well-arranged, decent, modest" (akin to *kosmos*, in its primary sense as "harmonious arrangement, adornment"; cf. *kosmikos*, of the world, which is related to

kosmos in its secondary sense as the world), is used in 1 Tim.
2:9 of the apparel with which Christian women are to adorn
themselves; in 3:2 (RV, "orderly;" KJV, "of good behavior"), .
. . "The well-ordering is not of dress and demeanor only, but of
the inner life, uttering indeed and expressing itself in the
outward conversation" (Trench, Syn., xcii).

Propriety (NKJ), Shamefacedness (KJV), Shamefastness (ASV)

aidos — "a sense of shame, modesty," is used regarding the
demeanor of women in the church, 1 Tim. 2:9 (some mss. have
it in Heb. 12:28 for *deos*, "awe": here only in NT). "Shamefastness is that modesty which is 'fast' or rooted in the character .
. . The change to 'shamefacedness' is the more to be regretted
because shamefacedness . . . has come rather to describe an
awkward diffidence, such as we sometimes call sheepishness"
(Davies, *Bible English*, p. 12).

Moderation (NKJ), Sobriety (KJV, ASV).

sophrosune — denotes "soundness of mind" . . . "it is that
habitual inner self-government, with its constant rein on all the
passions and desires, which would hinder the temptation to these
from arising."

D. *Christians should show that they are governed by chastity* —not
sensuality (1 Pet. 3:2). Thus, they try to conceal rather than
reveal their nakedness. The Bible associates shame with allowing
one's nakedness to appear (Rev. 3:18). Since the sin in the
garden of Eden, people have needed to be clothed so as to hide
their nakedness. "Nakedness" would, of course, apply to complete
nudity, but the term seems to be broader than that. The aprons or
loin coverings that Adam and Eve made for themselves were not
sufficient. Even Adam and Eve considered themselves naked with
these aprons. After having made them, they tried to hide from
God because they still considered themselves naked (Gen. 3:7-
10). Then God clothed them with coats of skins (v. 21). No
doubt, the aprons that they made would cover as much as things
commonly worn by both men and women, especially at the beach
or pool.

The breeches or trousers that priest were to wear, in addition
to their coats or tunics, were "to cover their nakedness; from the

loins even unto the thighs they shall reach" (Exod. 28:40-42).
The Pulpit Commentary in commenting on these breeches or
trousers says, "reaching from the waist to a little above the knee
... Unto the thighs —i.e., to the bottom of the thighs where they
adjoin the knees" (Vol. II, p. 293). It seems that the idea is that
both the loins and the thighs were to be covered. Hence, the
breeches reached from the waist down to the lower end of the
thighs. Josephus describes these breeches as "a girdle, composed
of fine twined linen, and is put about the privy parts, the feet
being to be inserted into them in the nature of breeches, but
above half of it is cut off, and it ends at the thighs, and is there
tied fast" (*Antiquities*, Book III, Chapter VII, Verse 1). If the
breeches were half cut of, it is evident that they were cut off at
the lower part of the thighs or at the knees. If the "unto the
thighs" means just reaching from the waist to the beginning of
the thighs then they would only reach to the hip joint. That seems
highly unlikely and borders on the absurd.

Would not chastity demand that we refrain from all seductive
gestures — including seductive clothing? When clothing reveals
too much it is seductive. It may be either too low, too high, too
brief, or too tight. Many popular fashions are seductive by
design.

E. *Christians should avoid being stumbling blocks* (Matt. 18:6-9). If
sensually seductive clothing does not present a stumbling block
to those of the opposite sex, it is hard to imagine anything being
a stumbling block. If it is wrong for one to "look to lust" (Matt.
5:28), then what about those who adorn themselves so as to
encourage such looking?

Conclusion

Christians can look nice and even contemporary without blindly
following the fashions of this world. They need to put more emphasis
upon the inward adorning than they do the outward (1 Pet. 3:1-4). Yet,
the outward adorning should reflect the godly nature of the inner man.

✍Briefly Answer

1. How should one be treated who attends church services in shabby

clothes? _____

2. What did Joseph do before appearing before Pharaoh? _____

_____

3. Define *modest, shamefastness,* and *sobriety.* _____

_____

_____

4. Why did God make coats for Adam and Eve? _____

5. What are some things reflected by one's fashions? _____

_____

✔Check "Yes" or "No"

1. Can we tell anything about a person's character by the way he dresses?

❒ Yes ❒ No

2. Does the Bible make any difference in the way that men and women

adorn themselves? ❒ Yes ❒ No

3. Should shame be associated with nakedness? ❒ Yes ❒ No

4. May one wear some clothes and still be considered "naked?" ❒ Yes

❒ No

5. Can one be fully clothed and be immodest? ❒ Yes ❒ No

✍Fill In The Blanks

1. "And, behold, there met him a woman with the attire of   an

_____, and subtil of heart" (Prov. 7:10).

2. "In like manner also, that women adorn themselves in _____

_____, with shamefacedness and sobriety; not with broided hair,

or gold, or pearls, or costly array; but (which becometh _____

_____ _____) with good works" (1 Tim. 2:9,10).

3. "Doth not even nature itself teach you, that, if a man have _____

hair, it is a _____ unto him? But if a woman have _____ hair,

it is a _____ to her. . ." (1 Cor. 11:14,15).

4. "And the Lord God called unto _____, and said unto him, Where

art thou? And he said, I heard thy voice in the garden, and I was

_____, because I was _____; and I hid myself"

(Gen. 3:9,10).

5. "Whose adorning let it not be that _____ adorning of plaiting the

hair, and of wearing of gold, or of putting on of apparel; But let it be

the _____ man of the _____, in that which is not corruptible,

even the ornament of a _____ and _____ spirit, which is in

the sight of God of great price " (1 Pet. 3:3,4).

For Class Discussion

1. Does 1 Peter 3:1-4 teach that it is wrong for a woman to wear jewelry?
   Give your reasons for your answer.
2. Discuss things that one's dress might signify about that person.

Lesson 9

The Selfishness Of This World

Introduction

Someone coined our present generation as the "me generation" referring to the unbridled selfishness that seems so prevalent. One should not be too surprised, seeing that the Bible puts selfishness at the head of the list of things that would come with perilous times in the last days: **"This know also, that in the last days perilous times shall come. For men shall be *lovers of their own selves,* covetous, boasters, proud, blasphemers, disobedient to parents, unthankful, unholy"** (2 Tim 3:1,2).

Selfishness belongs to the course of this world. It should be no part of the Christian's life. However, as it is with so many other things all around us, we have to be constantly vigilant lest we take up the ways of the world in this matter.

I.   The Course Of Our Lord: Self-sacrifice.

A. *Self-denial is essential to discipleship.* Jesus decreed, "If any man will come after me, let him deny himself, and take up his cross daily, and follow me" (Lk. 9:23). Again, "Whosoever he be of you that forsaketh not all that he hath, he cannot be my disciple" (Lk. 14:33).

It is not merely a matter of denying oneself *of things* or privileges, but a matter of denying *oneself.* It is self-crucifixion (Gal. 2:20; 5:24).

B. *Jesus is our perfect example of self-denial.* Being rich, He voluntarily became poor for us (2 Cor. 8:9). Being equal with God, He "made himself of no reputation, and took upon him the form of a servant" (Phil. 2:6,7). In view of this, we are to "let this mind be in you, which was in Christ Jesus" (v. 5), and "let nothing be done through strife or vainglory; but in lowliness of mind let each esteem others better than themselves" (v. 3). And,

"Look not every man to his own things, but every man also on the things of others" (v. 4). One simply cannot follow the Lord and be self-serving at the same time.

II. The Course Of This World: Self-service.

A. *Self-seeking, self-indulgence, and self-gratification* are too often considered normal behavior in this world. All too often, even when things seemingly are done to benefit others, they are really done out of self-interest. "For those who are such do not serve our Lord Jesus Christ, but their own belly, and by smooth words and flattering speech deceive the hearts of the simple" (Rom. 16:18, NKJ). "By covetousness they will exploit you with deceptive words" (2 Pet. 2:1, NKJ). "Therefore, when you do a charitable deed, do not sound a trumpet before you as the hypocrites do in the synagogues and in the streets, that they may have glory from men. Assuredly, I say to you, they have their reward" (Matt. 6:2, NKJ).

B. *Self-seeking leads to many other problems in this world.* "But if you have bitter envy and self-seeking in your hearts, do not boast and lie against the truth . . . For where envy and self-seeking exist, confusion and every evil thing are there" (Jas. 3:14-16, NKJ).

III. The Obsession With Exercising Personal Rights.

A. Judging from the news media, one gets the impression that nearly every person in the world is demanding his or her rights or those of his or her segment of society. In the matter of "rights," self-seeking abounds along with the accompanying confusion mentioned by James. Never mind what is best for society, neighbors, the family, the nation, or the Lord — *I must have my rights.* Never mind the confusion, strife, bitterness, and hatred that may be generated — *I must have my rights.* This may be the course of this world, but is it the course that a Christians should follow?

B. The Christian, being unselfish, is willing to sacrifice his rights, when expedient, for the general good of others and the Lord's cause. Paul, as an apostle and preacher, had the right to a wife and financial support for his preaching. However, the good of others and the cause of Christ took precedent over his exercising those basic rights (1 Cor. 9). He uses the fact that he did not always exercise his rights in order to teach the Corinthians that they need not always demand and exercise their right, as Christians, to eat certain meats. If circumstances were such that it would hinder the Cause or lead a brother to sin against his conscience — then they should sacrifice their right (read 1 Cor. 8-9). The Lord does not give us the right to exercise our rights to the real hurt and/or destruction of others.

IV. A Woman's Right To An Abortion?

A. Does a woman have the right to abort a baby because "it is her body to do with as she pleases"? She may have the *legal* right, but does she have the *moral* right? What about the right of the baby to be born and live its life? What about the rights of the father? What about the right of the Lord to have His will done? What about the principle of esteeming others better than oneself?

It is the view of this writer that the so-called "right to an abortion" is part and partial of the selfishness of this world. Self-indulgence often leads to unwanted pregnancy and then the self-seeking mother-to-be aborts because she does not want the burden of caring for that child. Yes, there are probably exceptions to this generalization, but we still charge that *selfishness* is at the root of most abortions.

1. In many cases, the baby is aborted because it would interfere with the mother's life-style. She might even have to put her career on hold or abandon it altogether. A child requires time and money that could be spent on other things the mother might want or even need.

2. Often, abortions are performed to keep the mother from having to face the consequences of her sinfulness. If the baby is conceived in fornication then the mother's sin would shortly be known to all. To protect herself from facing the consequences of the revelation of her sin, she opts to abort the child. This is another manifestation of selfishness.

B. Does any one have the right to summarily cause the death of another human being? Does calling it a "fetus" mitigate the circumstances? Who would say that anyone has the right to cause the death of a *baby*? Does calling the baby a "fetus" change things?

1. The Bible indicates that the living thing in a mother's womb

is indeed another human being. Job says that he and his servants were made in the womb (cf. Job 31:15). David recognized God's protection of him as a human being while he was still in his mother's womb (Psa. 139:13). Jesus was a "child" and a "babe" while still in Mary's womb. Mary was "found with child" early in her pregnancy (Matt. 1:18). Late in her pregnancy she was "great with child" (Lk. 2:5) John, the Baptist, was called a babe while in the womb of Elizabeth (Lk. 1:41). Jesus was called a babe out of the womb (Lk. 2:12). In or out of the womb, a babe is still a babe. Early or late in pregnancy, a child is still a child. What right does one have to kill a "babe" or a "child"? Call it a "fetus," if you like, the Bible still says it is a "child" or "babe." Would not the premeditated killing of a babe or a child be murder? If not, why not?

2. If one can destroy an unwanted human being while in the womb, why not those out of the womb? What about an undesirable child after it is born? What about adults who become a burden on their families and society because of health problems? Where does one stop "playing God" in these matters?

Conclusion

A Christian must "love thy neighbor as thyself" (Matt. 22:39). He is to "esteem others better than himself" (Phil. 2:3). He ought to be willing to even lay down his life for his brethren (1 Jn. 3:16). In view of this, how can we selfishly demand "our rights" to the point that others are hurt by it? How can men and women be such "lovers of themselves"?

✍Briefly Answer

1. What are the signs of perilous times? _____

_____

_____

2. Whom must we deny to follow Jesus? _____

3. Why did Jesus say that hypocrites did their charitable deeds? _____

4. What does one find where self-seeking exists? _____

_____

5. Why is abortion generally an act of selfishness? _____

_____

✔Check "Yes" or "No"

1. Can one be a disciple of Christ without forsaking all that he has?

❏ Yes ❏ No

2. Should one protect his own rights first and then the rights of others?

❏ Yes ❏ No

3. Should an unborn child have any rights? ❏ Yes ❏ No

4. Should one always exercise his God-given rights? ❏ Yes ❏ No

5. Is a "fetus" a human being with rights? ❏ Yes ❏ No

✍Fill In The Blanks

1. "Look not every man on his _____ _____, but every man also on the _____ __ _____" (Phil. 2:4).

2. "For where envy and _____ exist, _____ and every evil thing are there" (Jas. 3:16, NKJ).

3. "And it came to pass, that, when _____ heard the salutation of Mary, the _____ leaped in her womb; and _____ was filled with the Holy Ghost" (Lk. 1:41).

4. "Thou shalt love thy _____ as thyself" (Matt. 22:39).

5. "And he said unto all, If any man would come after me, let him deny

_____, and take up his _____ _____, and follow me"
(Lk. 9:23).

For Class Discussion

1. Discuss the circumstances under which a Christian should sacrifice his personal rights.
2. Discuss any problems that may come to mind associated with the abortion issue. For example, if destroying a "fetus" is not killing a human being, at what point does it cease to be a "thing" and become a human being?

Lesson 10

The Fornicators Of This World

Introduction

"I wrote unto you in an epistle not to company with fornicators: yet not altogether with **the fornicators of this world,** or with the covetous, or extortioners, or with idolaters; for then must ye needs go out of the world" (1 Cor 5:9,10).

Fornicators are "sexually immoral people" (NKJ). *Porneia* (fornication), *pornos* (fornicator), and *porneuo* (to commit fornication) are general terms that include all kinds of sexual immorality as is indicated by the generic term "sexual immorality" used in several translations. It includes adultery, homosexuality, and other kinds of sexually immoral conduct. Our English word "pornography" is rooted in this family of Greek words.

The world during the lifetime of our Lord and His apostles was filled with sexual immorality, especially the pagan world. However, the Hebrew nation had its problems with it too. Her history, as recorded in the Old Testament, will bear this out. One only has to be a casual observer to realize that our world today is filled with it and seems to be getting worse by the minute. Terms are invented in an effort to give it respectability, such as, "living together," "alternate life-style," etc., but it is still old-fashioned fornication with all its ugliness and condemnation.

I. Sex Is For Marriage.

The Bible makes it clear that marital sex is honorable and that sex outside of marriage is defiled.

A. The Hebrew writer contrasts the honorable with the defiled. "Marriage is honourable in all, and the bed undefiled: but whoremongers and adulterers God will judge" (Heb. 13:4). "Marriage should be honored by all, and the marriage bed kept pure, for God will judge the adulterer and all the sexually immoral" (NIV). It is either the undefiled bed of marriage or defiled bed of fornication. There are no other options given.

B. Paul gives but three options during the time of distress in 1 Corinthians 7:1-9. "Now concerning the things whereof ye wrote unto me: It is good for a man not to touch a woman. Nevertheless, to avoid fornication, let every man have his own wife, and let every woman have her own husband" (vv. 1-2). The options are (1) celibacy ("not to touch a woman"), (2) have a marriage partner, or (3) fornication. There are no other choices recorded. Only the first two are acceptable to the Lord.

II. Married Fornicators.

While it is generally true that sex between people married to each other is honorable, there are exceptions.

A. *Herod and Herodias were married* (Mk. 6:17). Yet, John told Herod, "It is not lawful for thee to have her" (Matt. 14:4). So, there is such a thing as an unlawful marriage. It is not honorable and the bed is defiled.

B. *Jesus makes it clear that the result of certain marriages is adultery.* "But I say unto you, That whosoever shall put away his wife, saving for the cause of fornication, causeth her to commit adultery: and whosoever shall marry her that is divorced committeth adultery" (Matt. 5:32). "And I say unto you, Whosoever shall put away his wife, except it be for fornication, and shall marry another, committeth adultery: and whoso marrieth her which is put away doth commit adultery" (Matt. 19:9). Only three kinds of people are considered in these verses: (1) One who puts away a partner for fornication and marries another, (2) one who puts away a partner for any other reason than fornication and marries another, and (3) a person who has been put away by another for whatever reason and marries another. Only one of the three has a right to the marriage bed — the one who puts away a partner for fornication and marries another. The others, even though they are *married*, are still committing adultery.

C. *It should also be clear that this marriage law applies to all men, not just Christians*, as some contend. Where there is no law there can be no sin (Rom. 4:15; 5:13). People in the world commit fornication and adultery (1 Cor. 5:10; 6:9-10). If God's marriage law does not apply to the world, then people in the world could not be guilty of "adultery," since, by definition, "adultery" presupposes a marriage law. An adulterer is one "who has unlawful intercourse with the spouse of another."[1] How could adultery be unlawful for the alien sinner — if God's marriage law does not apply to him? How could it be with the *spouse* of another if the marriage law does not apply in the world at large?

III. Homosexual Fornicators.
A. God's attitude toward homosexuality can be seen by reading the Old Testament.
   1. *The destruction of Sodom.* God destroyed Sodom, a city with the dubious distinction of having a sin named for it. The nature of her prevailing sin is learned from reading Genesis 19. On the eve of her destruction, two angels in the form of men were guests in the home of Lot, Abraham's nephew. That night, they Bible says, "The men of Sodom, both old and young, all the people from every quarter, surrounded the house. And they called to Lot and said to him, 'Where are the men who came to you tonight? Bring them out to us that we may know them *carnally'*" (vv. 4,5, NKJ). To protect his guests, Lot offered the men what I suppose he considered a lesser evil — his two virgin daughters. This did not appease this "gay" mob. God destroyed the city and until this day the very mention of its name reminds us of God's attitude toward homosexuality.
   2. In *the law of Moses*, homosexuality was a capital offense. "If a man also lie with mankind, as he lieth with a woman, both of them have committed an abomination: they shall surely be put to death; their blood shall be upon them" (Lev. 20:13).
B. Homosexuality is specifically condemned by New Testament writers.
   1. *It is a vile, shameful, and unnatural error.* "For this reason God gave them up to vile passions. For even their women exchanged the natural use for what is against nature. Likewise also the men, leaving the natural use of the woman, burned in their lust for one another, men with men committing what is shameful, and receiving in themselves the penalty of their

---

[1] *An Expository Dictionary Of New Testament Words.* W. E. Vine, p. 14.

error which was due" (Rom. 1:26,27).
2. *It is among those things that are worthy of death* (Rom. 1:26,27, 32).
3. *It will keep one from inheriting the kingdom of God.* "Neither fornicators, nor idolaters, nor adulterers, nor homosexuals, nor sodomites, nor thieves, nor covetous, nor drunkards, nor revilers, nor extortioners will inherit the kingdom of God" (1 Cor. 6:9,10, NKJ).

Conclusion

God made man a sexual being. It was His way of perpetuating His design that living things bring forth after their kind. God also made man a moral being with the ability to choose between right and wrong and gave him law to govern his choices.

In the beginning, He instituted marriage between man and woman for the happiness of mankind. It is in this institution that man is to seek and find sexual fulfillment. Other sexual relationships are illicit. One has the option of exercising the necessary self-control to live celibate or he can enter a lawful marriage and find fulfillment. There are no other acceptable options.

The world constantly glorifies fornication and offers opportunities by legions to commit it, but we must "flee" it in all its forms and, if guilty, repent of it to be saved eternally (1 Cor. 6:18).

✍Briefly Answer

1. What does the word *fornication* mean as it is used in the New Testament? _____

2. What will God do to all sexually immoral people if they do not repent?
_____

3. What three options did Paul give concerning marriage in 1 Corinthians 7:1-9? _____
_____

4. How can a divorced person marry another spouse without committing

adultery? _____

5. Why did God destroy Sodom? _____

✔Check "Yes" or "No"

1. Did Herod marry Herodias? ❐ Yes ❐ No

2. Can a fornicator be saved? ❐ Yes ❐ No

3. May one commit adultery with the person to whom he is married?

   ❐ Yes ❐ No

4. Did the law of Moses provide equal rights for homosexuals in the
   nation of Israel? ❐ Yes ❐ No

5. Does Christ's teaching on marriage and divorce apply to people of the
   world? ❐ Yes ❐ No

✎Fill In The Blanks

1. "Now concerning the things whereof ye wrote unto me: It is good for
   a man not to_____ a woman. Nevertheless, to avoid _____,
   let every man have his own_____, and let every woman have her
   own _____ " (1 Cor. 7:1,2).

2. "For John said unto him, It is not _____ for thee to have her"
   (Matt. 14:4).

3. "And I say unto you, Whosoever shall _____ _____ his wife,
   except it be for _____, and shall marry another, committeth
   _____ : and whoso marrieth her which is put away doth
   commit _____ " (Matt. 19:9).

4. "Because the law worketh wrath: for where no _____ is, there is no _____" (Rom. 4:15).

5. "Do you not know that the _____ will not inherit the _____ of God? Do not be deceived. Neither _____, nor idolaters, nor _____, nor _____, nor _____, nor thieves, nor covetous, nor drunkards, nor revilers, nor extortioners will inherit the _____ of God" (1 Cor. 6: 9,10, NKJ).

For Class Discussion

1. Discuss what one in an unlawful relationship must do in order to be saved.
2. Discuss "gay-rights" in view of biblical teaching on homosexuality.

Lesson 11

The Homes Of This World

Introduction

In this last half of the twentieth century, our society has developed concepts and expressions relating to home life that were hardly known just a few decades ago.

"Dysfunctional homes," "latchkey kids," "single parents," "house-husbands," and "alternate life styles" are heard often and accepted as normal. More and more children are forced to deal with two sets of parents — the mother and her husband and the father and his wife. Granted that some good people may be forced into some of these positions by forces over which they had no personal control, it still reflects a shift away from "traditional" family values in our society.

People living together and having a family without the benefit of marriage is treated as casually as "traditional" families. We even hear of "gay" marriages and "gay" parents with an adopted family.

The "traditional" home — where there is a father and mother married to each other with the father primarily making the living and the mother primarily devoted to home making—is still very much alive, but its strength is failing by the day. Christians need to be aware of what the Bible says about home life and seek to mold their homes accordingly rather that falling into the pattern that so often shapes the homes of this world.

I. The Single Parent Homes Boom.

A. *One parent homes are sometimes unavoidable.* This writer's grandmother was widowed at age 30 with five small children and never remarried. She raised her family on a hillside farm and taught them the work ethic and great family values based on God's word. A mother of five in Mississippi was divorced and forced out of her home by a well-to-do husband who objected to her faith and her bringing up their children in the faith. She raised and educated those children as well as anyone we have known. Nothing that we say about the single parent boom should reflect upon people like the ones in the above examples.

B. However, if we can believe the news reports, movies and television programs, *more and more singles are choosing to become parents.* Of course, to become parents these must commit fornication — a practice becoming too accepted in our society. In our last lesson, we showed that God will judge the fornicator unfavorably (Heb. 13:4). Some have chosen fornication, not wanting to be parents, but are now having to be single parents as a consequence of their choosing to sin.

C. *The soaring divorce rate produces many single parents.* According to the *U.S. National Center for Health Statistics,* there were 385,114 divorces in 1950 and 1,777,000 in 1990. Children become innocent victims of the misconduct of their parents. God hates divorce (Mal. 2:16). Jesus made it clear that it was not his will that people divorce for every cause (Matt. 19:1-9). As noticed in lesson ten, he gave only one cause for divorce that would free one to marry another.

II. Bible Teaching That Would Enrich Our Homes and Minimize Domestic Break Downs.

A. *Make real love.* There is no place for fornication in real love. "And walk in love, as Christ also hath loved us, and hath given himself for us an offering and a sacrifice to God for a sweet-smelling savour. But fornication, and all uncleanness, or covetousness, let it not be once named among you, as becometh saints" (Eph. 5:2,3). Notice that fornication is contrasted with "walking in love."

Real love is not the shallow passion depicted on soap operas or in fairy tales. It is a love that can be taught, learned, and consciously cultivated. It is commanded and can be obeyed. Husbands are commanded to love their wives (Eph. 5:25). Young women can be taught to love their husbands and children (Tit. 2:4). Real love is not something that just happens. One does not just fall into and out of it. It is something that one cultivates as a matter of principle. It demonstrates itself more by deed than by word: "My little children, let us not love in word, neither in tongue; but in deed and in truth" (1 Jn. 3:18; see also 1 Cor.

13:4-7). It is lasting because it is the result of conscious commit-
ment rooted in conviction rather than the mere sensational feeling
or passion of the moment.

B. *Follow the things which make for peace* (cf. Rom. 14:19). In the
marriage relationship, God has called us unto peace (1 Cor. 7:15).
Like love, to have peace, one must work at it. Peace requires
meekness, longsuffering, and forbearance (Eph. 4:2,3). The
absence of peace can make home life miserable, to say nothing
of causing it to break up. This is vividly pointed out in the
Proverbs: "It is better to dwell in the wilderness, than with a
contentious and an angry woman" (21:19). "It is better to dwell
in the corner of the housetop, than with a brawling woman and
in a wide house" (25:24). The family circle should never become
a fighting ring, but rather a haven of peace from the turmoil
already in the world.

C. *Consider one another.* Each partner in the marriage needs to be
considerate of the other's physical and emotional needs and
desires: "The husband should fulfill his marital duty to his wife,
and likewise the wife to her husband. The wife's body does not
belong to her alone but also to her husband. In the same way, the
husband's body does not belong to him alone but also to his
wife. Do not deprive each other except by mutual consent and for
a time, so that you may devote yourselves to prayer. Then come
together again so that Satan will not tempt you because of your
lack of self-control" (1 Cor. 7:2-5, NIV). Failure here results in,
but is no excuse for, infidelity and broken marriages. Often this
neglect comes from being too busy with other things. It must not
be so if the marriage is to thrive as it should.

Each needs to make it as easy as possible for the other to
fulfil his or her role in the home. The husband has the responsibility as head, ruler, and provider in the home (Eph. 5:23; 1 Tim.
3:5; 5:8). It is a great burden upon his shoulders. A wife helps
when she makes it as easy as possible for him to rule and
provide. The wife must submit to and obey her husband (1 Pet.
3:5; Eph. 5:22). She is to guide (manage) the house and be a
homemaker for her husband and children: "Therefore I desire that
the younger widows marry, bear children, manage the house, give
no opportunity to the adversary to speak reproachfully" (1 Tim.
5:14, NKJ). "That they admonish the young women . . . to be

discreet, chaste, **homemakers,** good, obedient to their own husbands, that the word of God may not be blasphemed" (Tit. 2:5, NKJ). In a society where homemaking is looked down upon by so many, a good husband needs to do all that he can to make his wife feel that her life is not wasted but rather honor her in word and deed for her willingness to fill this noble role (cf. 1 Pet. 3:7). Husbands, let her know how important her job is to you and to the Lord. This will go a long way in keeping the home at peace, functional, and in tact.

D. *A mutual respect for God and His way.* Many marriages have survived hard times because both parties wanted to please God. Divorce was out of the question because both parties knew and respected what the Bible teaches about it. So many of the New Testament's instructions on home responsibilities are re-enforced with an appeal to spiritual motives. Seek peace because *God* has called us to peace (1 Cor. 7:15). Love and submit like *Christ* and the *church* (Eph. 5:23-33). Behave in the home lest the *word of God* be blasphemed (Tit. 2:5). A wife is to have a quiet spirit "which is in the sight of *God* of great price" (1 Pet. 3:4). A husband is to treat his wife so that his *prayers* will not be hindered (1 Pet. 3:7). Parents are to bring their children up in the "training and admonition *of the Lord*" (Eph. 6:4, NKJ). Children are to obey their parents *in the Lord* (Eph. 6:1). The saying, "The family that prays together stays together," is not a bad idea at all.

Conclusion

If people would get back to the basics taught in the Bible, rather than following the course of this world, we would likely hear less about "dysfunctional homes," "latchkey kids," "single parents," "house-husbands," and "alternate life styles," don't you think?

✍Briefly Answer

1. What is God's attitude toward divorce? _____

2. What do older women need to teach younger women to do? _____

3. What are some things that help to enrich home life? _____

_____

4. According to Ephesians 4, what are some things that contribute to peace? _____

5. What are some things in our society that show a shift away from "traditional" family values? _____

✔Check "Yes" or "No"

1. Are one parent homes always a result of sin? ☐ Yes ☐ No

2. Can one express real love in fornication? ☐ Yes ☐ No

3. Does the Bible picture homemaking as a demeaning role for women?

☐ Yes ☐ No

4. Does the Bible teach wives to obey their husbands? ☐ Yes ☐ No

5. Does the Bible teach husbands to honor their wives? ☐ Yes ☐ No

✎Fill In The Blanks

1. "It is better to dwell in the _____, than with a _____ and an angry _____" (Prov. 21:19).

2. "That they admonish the young _____ to love their _____, to love their _____, to be discreet, chaste, _____, good, _____ to their own husbands, that the word of God may not be_____" (Tit. 2:4,5, NKJ).

3. "Likewise, ye _____, dwell with them according to _____, giving honour unto the wife, as unto the _____ vessel, and as being heirs together of the grace of life; that your

_____ be not hindered" (1 Pet. 3:7).

4. "For the _____ is the head of the wife, even as Christ is the head of the_____: and he is the _____ of the body" (Eph. 5:23).

5. "Husbands, _____ your wives, even as _____ also loved the _____, and gave _____ for it" (Eph. 5:25).

For Class Discussion

1. Describe homes that you would consider dysfunctional.
2. Discuss steps, based on scriptural principles, that couples might take to protect their homes from following the course of this world.

Lesson 12

The Dissipation Of This World

Introduction

Therefore, since Christ suffered for us in the flesh, arm yourselves also with the same mind, for he who has suffered in the flesh has ceased from sin, that he no longer should live the rest of his time in the flesh for the lusts of men, but for the will of God. For we have spent enough of our past lifetime in doing the will of the Gentiles — when we walked in lewdness, lusts, drunkenness, revelries, drinking parties, and abominable idolatries. In regard to these, they think it strange that you do not run with them in the same flood of dissipation, speaking evil of you (1 Pet. 4:1-4, NKJ).

In three places (Eph 5:18; Tit. 1:6; 1 Pet 4:4) where the King James and American Standard versions use either "riot" or "excess," later versions like the New King James and New International versions use the term "dissipation," "debauchery," or "wild." The word from which these words are translated (*asotia*) means "an abandoned, dissolute, life; profligacy, prodigality."[1] The adverb form is translated "riotous" (KJV, ASV), "wild" (NIV), and "prodigal" (NKJ).

In 1 Peter 4:4, it is obvious that this word is a general word covering many specifics like those listed in verse three. Dissipation or debauchery manifests itself in many specific forms in this present world.

I. Alcohol and Other Drug Abuse.

A. *There is a legitimate use of alcohol and other drugs.* Few would deny this. Paul urged Timothy to drink a "little wine" for his stomach and often infirmities (1 Tim. 5:23). After indicating that wine and strong drink was not good for kings and princes, "Lest

---

[1] *Greek-English Lexicon Of The New Testament*, Joseph Henry Thayer, p. 82.

they drink, and forget the law, and pervert the judgment of any of the afflicted," the writer says, "Give strong drink unto him that is ready to perish, and wine unto those that be of heavy heart" (Prov. 31:6,7). This seems to indicate the medical use of alcohol as a pain reliever and as a sedative.

B. *There is much evidence against various kinds of alcohol and drug abuse in the Scriptures.*

1. Our text (1 Pet. 4:1-4) lists *drunkenness and drinking parties* among the specific forms of dissipation. Most Christians agree that drunkenness is sinful. However, many argue that "social" or recreational drinking is permissible and even harmless. The word translated "banquetings" (KJV) and "carousings" (ASV, NIV) is translated "drinking parties" in the New King James. Both Thayer and Vine says the word (*potos*) literally means "a drinking."

It is well known that alcohol impairs reason, will, self-control, judgment, physical skills, and endurance. A Christian is to be sober-minded (Tit. 2:4-6; 1 Pet 1:13). A drinker impairs his ability to maintain sober-mindedness. In Titus 2:6, the New International Version has "self-controlled" rather than *sober* or *sober-minded*." When one alters his mind with mind-impairing drugs such as alcohol, he is to some degree, surrendering the ability to control himself.

Lately, many in the world are beginning to recognize the harm done by social drinking. "If you drink, don't drive" is a widely used slogan these days. Alcohol's effect upon one's health is beginning to be emphasized more and more by those in the health-care field. In view of all of this, why should a Christian want to drink at all? Even people of the world are beginning to see that it is not as harmless as they once thought it was.

Efforts to justify modern social drinking by the wine drinking of the Bible fall short when one looks at the facts closely. One would need to prove that the wine innocently drunk in the Bible was parallel to the drink used by the social drinker today. While "wine" (Gr. *oinos*) often refers to a drink with intoxicating quality, it does not always do so. It, in reference to the grape, is kind of like our English word, "cider" in reference to apples — a word used of the juice of the apple ranging from fresh apple juice all the way to "hard cider" or fully fermented apple juice. Isaiah speaks of "wine . . . found in the cluster" (Isa. 65:8). Josephus (*Antiquities of the Jews*, Book II, Chapter V, Verse 2) illustrates how the word "wine" was used in ancient times: "He therefore said, that in his sleep he saw three clusters of grapes hanging upon three branches of a vine, large already, and ripe for gathering; and that he squeezed them into a cup which the king held in his hand; and when he had strained *the wine*, he gave it to the king to drink" (Italics mine, eob). This ancient writer calls freshly squeezed grape juice *wine*.

Even if one granted that all "wine" in the Bible was of the fermented variety, there is much evidence that it does not parallel the fortified wines used today to say nothing of the stronger alcoholic beverages used by social drinkers. When the alcohol of natural fermentation of grape juice reaches about 14% it kills the yeast which is the fermenting agent in the juice and the fermentation stops. Often the process is stopped before reaching the 14% level. Note the following excerpt from *Bible Wines* by William Patton concerning the ancient practice of mixing water with wine.

> There is abundance of evidence that the ancients mixed their wines with water; not because they were so strong with alcohol, as to require dilution, but because, being rich syrups, they needed water to prepare them for drinking. The quantity of water was regulated by the richness of the wine and time of year.
>
> "Those ancient authors who treat upon domestic manners abound with allusions to this usage. Hot water, tepid water, or cold water was used for the dilution of wine according to the season." "Hesiod prescribed, during the summer months, three parts of water to one of wine." "Nicochares considers two parts of wine to five of water the proper proportion." "According to Homer, Pramnian and Meronian wines required twenty parts water to one of wine. Hippocrates considered twenty parts of water to one of the Thracian wine to be the proper beverage" . . . — *Bible Commentary*, p. 17.

2. Galatians 5:20 lists "witchcraft" (KJV) or "sorcery" (NKJ) as

a work of the flesh. The word (Gr. *pharmakeia*) has reference to the use of drugs by sorcerers in their work. Our English word *pharmacy* comes from the same word. The harmful and evil effects of drug abuse are becoming so widely known, that it seems hardly necessary to argue the case against it for those who want to live "soberly, righteously, and godly in this present world." Even though the social and recreational use of alcohol and drugs is not specified in the list of works of the flesh, it certainly would be covered by the "such like" in verse 21.

II. Lewdness, Lusts and Related Matters.

Lewdness (KJV) or lasciviousness (NKJ) is a work of the flesh (Gal. 5:19). It is a form of dissipation (1 Pet. 1:3). In lesson eight we discussed this word as it applies to our dress and appearance. In this lesson we want to briefly note some other lewdness and lust.

A. *Lewd and lustful literature.* All forms of public media depict lewdness and lust as innocent. Pornography ("hard" and "soft"), words and pictures that cause lust, are readily available to any who desires it in magazines, movies and TV programming. Small segments of it are often slipped into otherwise wholesome pieces of literature and entertainment and sprung upon those who do not want it. Christians must constantly guard their minds to be sure that their thinking is wholesome (cf. Phil. 4:8).

B. *Lewd and lustful language* in ordinary conversation. A Christian is admonished to "let no corrupt communication proceed out of your mouth" (Eph. 4:29). Vulgarity and profanity must not characterize a Christian's speech.

C. *Lewd and lustful activity.* Modern dances are prime examples of this kind of activity. They promote lust either by the close contact between male and female (not married to each other) or by those dances that stir lust by visual means where there is little or no physical contact. Remember Thayer defines "lasciviousness" or "lewdness" as "indecent bodily movements, unchaste handling of males and females" (pp. 79,80).

Yes, the Bible does speak of dances in a favorable light (Exod. 15:20; Judg. 11:34; 1 Sam. 18:6; Lk. 15:25 and other passages). Solomon even said there is a time to dance (Eccl. 3:4). These dances expressed joy and gratitude for victories or favors bestowed on them by God. The dances that praised God belonged to the Old Testament age. Nowhere are such authorized in the New Testament. They were by men and women dancing alone — not mixed.

There is no way that those dances approved in the Bible can be equated with the dances of this age. Anyone who knows anything about the sexual nature of man knows that the modern dances are designed to appeal to man's base sensuality.

Conclusion

Those who refuse to run with the world "in the same flood of dissipation" can expect the world to think them strange even speaking evil of them. It goes with the territory. We must learn that it is far more important to do the will of God than to be accepted and/or praised by our neighbors in the world. Our lives must be lived so as to contribute to man's improvement rather than to his dissipation. Dissipation may be the course of this world, but Christians, while in the world, are not of the world.

✍Briefly Answer

1. Define *dissipation*. _____

2. What are legitimate uses of alcohol and other drugs? _____

_____

3. What are some dangers of "social drinking"? _____

_____

4. What forms of lewdness do we encounter daily? _____

_____

5. How does Thayer define *lasciviousness* or *lewdness*? _____

_____

✔Check "Yes" or "No"

1. Does the word *banqueting* in the KJV mean merely having a large

formal meal? ❏ Yes ❏ No

2. Did Bible "wine" *always* contain alcohol? ❏ Yes ❏ No

3. Was drug abuse associated with *sorcery?* ❏ Yes ❏ No

4. Should a Christian let corrupt communication come out of his mouth?
❏ Yes ❏ No

5. Does the Bible condone all kinds of dancing? ❏ Yes ❏ No

✍Fill In The Blanks

1. "In regard to these, they think it _____ that you do not run with
them in the same flood of _____, speaking evil of you"
(1 Pet. 4:4, NKJ).

2. "For we have spent enough of our past lifetime in doing the will of
the _____ — when we walked in _____, lusts,
_____, revelries, _____ _____, and abominable
idolatries" (1 Pet. 4:3, NKJ).

3. "Now the works of the _____ are manifest, which are these;
_____, fornication, uncleanness, _____" (Gal. 5:19).

4. "Thus saith the Lord, As the new wine is found in the _____, and
one saith, Destroy it not; for a blessing is in it: so will I do for my
servants' sakes, that I may not destroy them all" (Isa. 65:8).

5. "Wherefore gird up the loins of your mind, be _____, and hope
to the end for the grace that is to be brought unto you at the
_____ of Jesus Christ" (1 Pet. 1:13).

For Class Discussion

1. Discuss the harmful effects of all kinds of drug abuse, including alcohol, on individuals, society, families, and the church.
2. Discuss the various forms of lasciviousness in our society today.

The Dispositions Of This World

Introduction

A Christian needs to be careful to be right both in *position* and in *disposition*. It is not enough to hold all the correct doctrinal positions, one must show the right dispositions in his life. Nor is it enough to demonstrate a righteous disposition, one must also be sure that his positions will stand the test of God's word.

The works of the flesh (Gal. 5:19-21) contain several items of what is commonly called "worldliness." Some items have to do with base sensuality ("adultery, fornication, uncleanness, lasciviousness"), some with religious error and superstition ("idolatry, witchcraft [sorcery]"), some with debauchery ("drunkenness, revellings"), at least one with acts of violence ("murders") and some with attitudes or dispositions ("hatred" through "envyings"). Many of us who are not guilty of base sensuality, superstition, debauchery nor any kind of violence may find ourselves up to our necks in the sins of disposition. These sins of disposition are also worldly and soul-destroying.

I. Hatred.

This word (Gr. *echthra*) means hostility or enmity. It is translated "enmity" in Luke 23:12; Romans 8;7; Ephesians 2:15-16 and James 4:4. In Galatians 5:20 it is translated "enmities" in the American Standard. Vine says. "It is the opposite of *agape*, love." Someone has said, and I think rightly so, that *agape* is "active good will toward its object." If that is the case, then hatred must be active ill will toward its object. A Christian cannot afford to harbor enmity even against an enemy (Matt. 5:43,44). In view of this, how can we afford hatred toward a brother (1 Jn. 2:9,11; 3:15; 4:20)?

II. Variance.

This word (Gr. *eris*) means "strife" (ASV), "discord" (NIV), or "contentions" (NKJ). It is twice translated "debate" in the King James (Rom. 1:29; 2 Cor. 12:20), leading some to conclude that all debating is sinful — especially debating religious differences. Albert Barnes does a good job of putting the word into perspective: "Our common word *debate* does not commonly imply evil. It denotes commonly *discussion* for elucidating truth; or for maintaining a proposition, as the *debates* in Parliament, &c. But the word in the original meant also *contention, strife,* altercation, connected with anger and heated zeal."[1]

It is a disposition that lends itself to altercations with others. A Christian, rather than seeking altercations, is to "as much as lieth in you, live peaceably with all men (Rom. 12:18).

III. Emulations.

This word (Gr. *zelos*) is used both favorably and unfavorably in the New Testament. It means "properly, heat, i.e. (figuratively) 'zeal' (in a favorable sense, ardor; in an unfavorable one, jealousy, as of a husband [figuratively, of God], or an enemy, malice)" (*Strong's Greek Dictionary*). Other translations of this verse render it *jealousy* or *jealousies.*

"Set me as a seal upon thine heart, as a seal upon thine arm: for love is strong as death; jealousy is cruel as the grave: the coals thereof are coals of fire, which hath a most vehement flame" (Song of Sol. 8:6). How can we really "rejoice with them that do rejoice" (Rom. 12:15) with a disposition prone toward jealousy?

IV. Wrath.

This word (Gr. *thumos*) carries with it the idea of heated anger that expresses itself in "fits of rage" (NIV) or "outbursts of wrath" (NKJ). It is the disposition that we sometimes call "hot tempered" or "hot headed." Colloquially it is often referred to as "flying off the handle." Standing opposite to this disposition, in the fruit of the Spirit, is "temperance" or "self-control" (v. 23).

V. Strife.

This word (Gr. *eritheia*) is sometimes translated "selfish ambitions" (NKJ, NIV) and "factions" (ASV). Of this word, Vine comments, "It is derived, not from *eris*, 'strife,' but from *erithos*, 'a hireling,' hence the

---

[1] *Barnes on the New Testament, Romans,* p. 51.

meaning of 'seeking to win followers,' 'faction,' so rendered in the RV of 2 Cor. 12:20, KJV, 'strifes"; not improbably the meaning here is rivalries, or base ambitions."[1] It is that self seeking ambition that results in parties or factions. A Christian is to work out of a desire for the good of others in general and the church in particular rather than seeking a personal following to serve his own selfish designs. It is the kind of disposition that leads to a "Diotrephes" (read 3 Jn. 9-10).

VI. Seditions.

This word (Gr. *dichostasia*) literally means "a standing apart."[2] It is also translated "dissensions" (NKJ, NIV) or "divisions" (ASV). Those who cause divisions contrary to the doctrine of Christ are to be marked and avoided (Rom. 16:17). The next verse (18) suggests that such are self-serving. Again, we are talking about a disposition or an attitude problem.

VII. Heresies.

This word (Gr. *hairesis*) is "parties" (ASV) or "factions" (NIV) in some translations. In application it is closely aligned with the two previous words. It is "'an opinion,' especially a self-willed opinion, which is substituted for submission to the power of truth, and leads to division and the formation of sects, Gal. 2:20 (marg. 'parties'); such erroneous opinions are frequently the outcome of personal preference or the prospect of advantage."[3] A heretic or factious man is one who is "causing division by a party spirit"[4] and needs to be rejected after the first and second admonition (Tit. 3:10).

VIII. Envyings.

This word (Gr. *phthonos*) refers to "the feeling of displeasure produced by witnessing or hearing of the advantage or prosperity of others. . . *Zelos*, 'zeal or jealousy,' translated 'envy' in the KJV, in Acts 13:45 . . . is to be distinguished from *phthonos*, and, apart from the

---

[1] *An Expository Dictionary Of New Testament Words*, W. E. Vine, pp. 220, 221.
[2] *Ibid.* p. 556.
[3] *Ibid*, p. 303.
[4] *Ibid.*

meaning of 'zeal' and 'indignation,' is always translated 'jealousy' in the RV. The distinction lies in this, that 'envy' desires to deprive another of what he has, 'jealousy' desires to have the same or the same sort of thing for itself."[1]

Solomon wrote that envy is "the rottenness of the bones" (Prov. 14:30). Envy on the part of the Jewish leaders was a factor in the crucifixion of Jesus (Matt. 27:18). It caused Joseph's brothers to sell him into Egypt (Acts 7:9).

Conclusion

Christians must constantly guard their attitudes or dispositions against being overly influenced by the attitudes of those who follow "the course of this world." We are to "walk in the Spirit, and ye shall not fulfil the lust of the flesh" (Gal. 5:16). One does this when he walks according to the teachings of the Spirit given to us in the Apostles' word revealed to them by the Spirit (Eph. 3:5). The fruit of such a walk is the disposition called the "fruit of the Spirit" (Gal. 5:22-23), the opposite of "the works of the flesh."

✎Briefly Answer

1. What "works of the flesh" are associated with one's disposition? ___

2. What is the difference between jealousy and envy? ___

3. What is a heretic? ___

4. What should be done with one who causes divisions? ___

5. What does *debate*, as used in the King James New Testament, mean?

---

[1] *Ibid.* p. 204.

✔Check "Yes" or "No"

1. Should one hate his enemies? ☐ Yes ☐ No

2. Does the word of God forbid all kinds of religious debating? ☐ Yes ☐ No

3. Does *heresies* refer to self-willed opinions? ☐ Yes ☐ No

4. Did envy have anything to do with the Lord's death? ☐ Yes ☐ No

5. Is one right because he always has a good attitude? ☐ Yes ☐ No

✐Fill In The Blanks

1. "Now the works of the flesh are manifest, which are these; adultery, fornication, uncleanness, lasciviousness, Idolatry, witchcraft, _____, _____, _____, _____, _____, _____, _____, _____, murders, drunkenness, revellings, and _____ _____: of the which I tell you before, as I have also told you in time past, that they which do such things shall not inherit the _____ of _____ " (Gal. 5:19-21).

2. "But the fruit of the _____ is love, joy, _____, longsuffering, _____, goodness, faith, meekness, _____: against such there is no law" (Gal. 5:22-23).

3. "If it be possible, as much as lieth in _____, live _____ with all _____" (Rom. 12:18).

4. "Whosoever _____his _____ is a murderer: and ye know that no murderer hath _____ _____abiding in him"

(1 Jn. 3:15).

5. "_____ (is) the rottenness of the bones" (Prov. 14:30).

For Class Discussion

1. Discuss each wrong disposition or attitude in this lesson and ways to help eliminate each sinful disposition from our lives.
2. Discuss additional sins that might grow out of each wrong attitude studied in this lesson.

www.ingramcontent.com/pod-product-compliance
Lightning Source LLC
Chambersburg PA
CBHW060035050426
42448CB00012B/3025